Thomas Mann's
Death in Venice

Thomas Mann's
Death in Venice

A Reference Guide

ELLIS SHOOKMAN

Greenwood Guides to Literature

GREENWOOD PRESS
Westport, Connecticut • London

Library of Congress Cataloging-in-Publication Data

Shookman, Ellis.
    Thomas Mann's *Death in Venice*: a reference guide / Ellis Shookman.
        p. cm. — (Greenwood guides to literature)
    ISBN 0–313–31159–5 (alk. paper)
        1. Mann, Thomas, 1875–1955. Tod in Venedig.   2. Mann, Thomas, 1875–1955—Criticism
    and interpretation.   I. Title.   II. Series.
    PT2625.A44Z7955   2004
    833'.912—dc22   2003056800

British Library Cataloguing in Publication Data is available.

Library of Congress Catalog Card Number: 2003056800
ISBN: 0–313–31159–5
ISSN: 1543–2262

First published in 2004

Greenwood Press, 88 Post Road West, Westport, CT 06881
An imprint of Greenwood Publishing Group, Inc.
www.greenwood.com

Printed in the United States of America

The paper used in this book complies with the
Permanent Paper Standard issued by the National
Information Standards Organization (Z39.48–1984).

10 9 8 7 6 5 4 3 2 1

Contents

Preface

This book is meant to introduce students and general readers alike to one of the most beautiful and powerful works of fiction ever written: Thomas Mann's *Death in Venice* (1912). It is also intended to help them go beyond the superficial level of Mann's plot and discover the literary and intellectual qualities that make his famous story so rich and so rewarding. These qualities are stylistic, cultural, historical, philosophical, and psychological. Appreciating them enables one to avoid simplistic, crude, or distorted interpretations of Mann's text. Such interpretations are common, thanks partly to the popularity of Luchino Visconti's *Morte a Venezia* (1971). This film is a fine example of cinematic art, an admirable creation in its own right, but it tells a different story than Mann's novella, its primary source, and the two works should not be confused. Such misinterpretations also abound for other reasons. One such reason is that English translations of *Death in Venice*—in German, *Der Tod in Venedig*—can never render the subtleness of Mann's prose. As a result, those translations lose narrative nuances that make all the difference when deciding what the novella may mean. Another reason is that Mann describes a homoerotic attraction. Some critics ignore this fact; others overreact to it. Some find it repulsive; others consider it liberating. The novella itself is actually far more complex and ambiguous than such critical extremes might lead one to believe. Indeed, understanding it well requires close reading and careful attention to details. Such reading and attention reveal its larger issues. They also make it enjoyable. The purpose of the present study, then, is to help readers savor as well as comprehend one of Mann's challenging masterpieces.

The scope and organization of this study reflect that purpose. Its topics, like Mann's, range from history, culture, and philosophy to psychology and literary style. These and other topics are closely linked in Mann's story. Here they are considered in eight separate chapters. Chapter 1 gives an overview of Mann's life and works before comparing *Death in Venice* to some of his other short fiction and to works by other writers. This introduction treats the novella as one part of his long career as well as from the broad perspective of world literature. Chapter 2 gives a general introduction to each of Mann's five chapters as well as a detailed summary of the events that they relate. The contents of the novella are here presented as fully as possible. Chapter 3 examines the genesis and the editions of *Death in Venice*. This discussion of Mann's text considers one of his own trips to Venice, some of his letters, and his working notes. It also considers German editions of that text, and it compares all of the English translations. Chapter 4 regards the historical, cultural, and sociological factors that figure in Mann's story, as well as literary and other influences. It treats contexts such as the First World War and the career of Frederick the Great as well as Prussianism, Protestantism, and modernism. It also discerns literary influences from modern Germany and France as well as ancient Greece, not to mention other influences. Chapter 5 presents pairs of ideas: Dionysus and the Dionysian, knowledge and Mann's notion of "reborn naiveté," aestheticism and decadence, pederasty and homoeroticism, and sexual dreams and civilized discontent. These ideas underlie the events that Mann describes and lend them deeper meaning. Chapter 6 considers Mann's narrative art: his choices of verbs and nouns, his repetition of various elements, his symbols and images, and his often ironic point of view. Understanding these narrative features is crucial to making sense of his story. Chapter 7 reviews the reception of that story, explaining all the most important approaches that critics have taken to it. Chapter 8 lists and briefly describes the major reviews and scholarly studies of the novella. Both of these last two chapters show what other, professional readers have made of Mann's story. May they and the six preceding them inspire their readers' own, new, informed interpretations.

The value of this book as a reference guide, in fact, lies in the uses that readers can make of the information it provides. After discovering the comparisons drawn in chapter 1, they may be moved to read *Death in Venice* together with Mann's *Der kleine Herr Friedemann* (Little Herr Friedemann, 1897), *Gladius Dei* (1902), *Tristan* (1903), and *Tonio Kröger* (1903). They may also want to read it alongside works of fiction by other authors, works that were written before or after it in English, Italian, French, German, or Japanese. The extensive account of Mann's plot that is given in chapter 2 may help readers discuss his modes of reality, his hero's biography, the dramatic or even tragic elements in his story, his allusions to Greek mythology, and his ambiguous last scene. The history of how Mann wrote his novella and the details about its editions given in chapter 3 may help readers understand his hero's complexity as well as the subtleness of his literary language. This chapter may also help them choose an English translation. The international situation and the intellectual environment treated in chapter 4 may help readers relate Mann's story to issues dating not only from the late nineteenth or early twentieth centuries, but from eighteenth-century Germany and ancient Greece as well. The philosophical, literary, and psychoanalytic concepts considered in chapter 5 may aid readers who need to know how Mann's major issues and themes are still current today. Those issues and themes involve several eternally recurring human problems. The stylistic and structural features examined in chapter 6 may help readers see both how well Mann's story is made and why it qualifies as a work of verbal, literary art. The main critical methods surveyed in chapter 7 may be useful to readers who are interested in knowing how a single text can be explained from many angles and in many different ways. The reviews and studies cited in chapter 8 may similarly help readers see what can be made of Mann's story and how variously it can be interpreted, depending on one's standpoint, tastes, and ideas. The value of the present study would be greatest, though, if English-speaking readers were so impressed by its subject that they learned to read *Death in Venice* in the original German. Mann's story would then speak to them eloquently for itself.

Acknowledgments

For their help with the production of this book, I would like to thank
George F. Butler, Senior Editor, Greenwood Press, as well as Professor
Bruce Duncan and Professor Steven P. Scher, both of Dartmouth College.
I would also like to thank Laurie Wallach and to dedicate this book to
my parents.

Unless otherwise noted, all translations from Mann's German are mine.

1   Introduction

Mann wrote *Death in Venice* at a particular stage of his long life and his literary career. The meaning of the novella emerges more clearly, in fact, when one knows something about his biography and his other writings. Both figure in his story. In certain respects, and to a certain degree, his life was like that of its hero. His six main novels raise many of its issues, moreover, and his other works sometimes shed further light on its events. Four of his earlier novellas help explain *Death in Venice* especially well: *Der kleine Herr Friedemann* (Little Herr Friedemann, 1897), *Gladius Dei* (1902), *Tristan* (1903), and *Tonio Kröger* (1903). They, too, often describe the eruption of suppressed desire, the dubious morality of aestheticism, and a decadent author's attitude toward bourgeois life. They also help interpret its initial setting of Munich, the disease that it discusses, and its implicit links to the operatic composer Richard Wagner (1813–83). All four of these novellas are included in two of the more recent English collections of Mann's major stories, those translated by David Luke (1988) and Joachim Neugroschel (1998).[1] Readers who use one of these collections, which also include *Death in Venice*, can thus consult them easily. Mann's story can also be compared to works by other authors. It is similar both to Euripides' *Bacchae* and to Johann Wolfgang von Goethe's *Wahlverwandtschaften* (Elective Affinities, 1809), for instance, two texts often cited as influences on Mann and, accordingly, discussed in chapters 4 and 5 below. It is also similar to additional texts, especially to modern fiction written before or after it. Among that fiction written prior to it are works by Oscar Wilde (1854–1900), Joseph Conrad (1857–1924),

Gabriele D'Annunzio (1863–1938), André Gide (1869–1951), Henry James (1843–1916), and Mann's brother Heinrich (1871–1950). Fiction that is similar and subsequent to Mann's tale includes novels by James Joyce (1882–1941), Hermann Broch (1886–1951), Yukio Mishima (1925–70), Wolfgang Koeppen (1906–96), Vladimir Nabokov (1899–1977), Max Frisch (1911–91), and Ian McEwan (1948–). *Death in Venice* resembles these other works of fiction in various ways, and comparing it to them can help readers understand its story as well as its significance in world literature.

MANN'S LIFE AND WORKS

Mann's life was long and eventful. In some respects, it was also like the fictional life of Gustav von Aschenbach, the protagonist of *Death in Venice*. Mann was born on 6 June 1875 in the northern German city of Lübeck. His father was a successful merchant from a prominent family. His mother came from Brazil. His father died in 1891, and his mother soon moved to Munich with three of his four siblings. Mann left high school in 1894 without fully graduating. He, too, then moved to Munich, where he worked for an insurance company and audited courses at the Technical University. With his older brother Heinrich—like Thomas, an author—he wrote for a right-wing journal. The two brothers traveled and lived in Italy in the late 1890s. In 1898, back home in Munich, he worked for *Simplicissimus*, a satirical magazine. In 1900, he briefly served in a Bavarian infantry regiment. He became engaged to Katia Pringsheim in 1904, and they married a year later. By 1919, they would have six children. In 1908, Mann had a summerhouse built in a nearby spa, Bad Tölz. In 1910, his sister Carla committed suicide. In 1911, he vacationed in Venice with Katia and Heinrich. Starting in 1915, the two brothers were estranged by their strong personal and political differences. Thomas supported the German cause in the First World War, while Heinrich argued against it. They would reconcile in 1922, when Thomas, too, came out in favor of the democratic Weimar Republic. In 1919, he received an honorary doctorate from the University of Bonn. In 1927, his other sister, Julia, also committed suicide. In 1929, he won the Nobel Prize for Literature. It was awarded for his first novel, *Buddenbrooks* (1901). In 1933, after Hitler came to power, Mann did not return to Germany from a trip abroad, and he never resided permanently there again. Starting in 1934, he made several trips to the United States. In 1935, he received an honorary doctorate from Harvard and was a guest of President Franklin D. Roosevelt. In 1936, his German citizenship and his degree from the University of Bonn were both revoked, and he became a citizen of Czechoslovakia. By way of France, he came to the United States in 1938. He then held a professorship at Princeton, where he received another honorary doctorate in 1939. Beginning in 1940, he wrote speeches that the BBC broadcast to Germany. In 1941, he moved to Pacific Palisades, California. In 1944, he became an American citizen. In 1949, his oldest son Klaus, too, committed suicide. In the same year, 1949, Mann visited East as well as West Germany and was made an honorary citizen of Weimar, the city where Johann Wolfgang von Goethe (1749–1832), Germany's greatest literary figure, spent most of his life. Mann returned to Europe in 1952, moving to Switzerland. His hometown of Lübeck made him an honorary citizen not long before he died on 12 August 1955 in Zurich. Some of these biographical facts recur in his story. Like Mann, Aschenbach is a famous author from a well-established family. He, too, has a relatively exotic mother, moves to Munich, has traveled in Italy, owns a summerhouse in the mountains, and vacations in Venice. He was married as well, although his wife has died, as was not the case with Mann. Most other details of Aschenbach's life likewise differ from those of Mann's. Many are purely fictional.

Like Mann's life, many of his other writings are related to *Death in Venice* and often help explain it. Knowing about them, too, helps one make sense of his story. Major issues raised in that story also occur in his six main novels. *Buddenbrooks* (1901) relates the decline and fall of a wealthy bourgeois family very much like Mann's own. In four generations, and in just over forty years, the Buddenbrooks lose not only their will to succeed in business but also their will to live. They also take increasing interest in intellectual and artistic endeavors, though, so their decadence is complex. Cultural refinement comes at the expense of vitality, and the last in their line dies of typhoid fever. Progressive decadence and symbolic disease similarly figure in *Death in Venice*. Mann initially planned his next main novel, *Der Zauberberg* (The Magic Mountain, 1924), as a humoristic counterpart to this somber novella. It, too, ties disease—it is set in a Swiss sanatorium that treats tuberculosis—to heightened intellectual awareness, relating its hero's reflections on life and death to social and historical forces at work on the eve of the First World War. It also often alludes to Hermes. Those forces and this Greek god likewise inform *Death in Venice*. Mann's *Joseph und seine Brüder* (Joseph and His Brothers, 1933–43) consists of four novels that, among other things, describe a consciousness of myth. They greatly expand the biblical account of Jacob and his son

Joseph given in Genesis, chapters 27–50. Potiphar's wife, for example, is married to a eunuch, and the handsome Joseph accidentally awakens her repressed sexual desire. *Death in Venice* examines this same consciousness and this kind of desire. *Lotte in Weimar* (1939) embellishes an episode in the life of Goethe, whom it describes as a dignified artist remote from regular human existence. Mann claimed that he originally intended to retell another episode from the life of Goethe in *Death in Venice*, and Aschenbach, too, is a venerable yet isolated artist. *Doktor Faustus* (1947) updates Goethe's and others' tales of the learned man who sold his soul to the devil. It tells of an artist, a composer, whose creative difficulties hint at problems and dangers of Germanness, above all at the relapse into irrationality that resulted in National Socialism. This composer's music is sensuous and abstract, his symbolic disease is syphilis, and his life parallels that of the philosopher Friedrich Nietzsche (1844–1900). *Death in Venice*, too, describes an artist torn between sensuality and abstraction, links his death to an infectious disease, and has to do with Nietzsche, whose *Die Geburt der Tragödie* (The Birth of Tragedy, 1872) is the source of some of the concepts it treats. Finally, *Bekenntnisse des Hochstaplers Felix Krull* (Confessions of the Con Man Felix Krull, 1954) recasts Mann's life-long concern with artists' morality. He raises this concern in *Death in Venice* as well. In fact, he interrupted his work on *Felix Krull*, which remained unfinished, to write this novella in 1911. Mann's main novels thus shed light on the issues that the novella addresses. In its second chapter, Mann even alludes to *Buddenbrooks* and *Felix Krull*, implying that Aschenbach wrote them.

Some of Mann's further writings similarly help understand the fictional events described in *Death in Venice*. Those writings include a drama, two other novels, many other works of fiction, numerous essays, and various speeches. The novella alludes to some of them as well. In fact, Mann attributes to Aschenbach four publications that he himself planned but never wrote, at least not in the form that he initially intended. His unsuccessful drama *Fiorenza* (1907) stages a heated debate between representatives of religious morality and aesthetic enjoyment. These spokesmen—the Dominican monk Girolamo Savonarola (1452–98) and the Renaissance politician and patron of the arts Lorenzo de' Medici (1449–92)—argue about the opposition of intellect to life, art, and beauty. *Death in Venice* revisits the terms of this same antithesis. In its second chapter, moreover, Mann alludes to both these characters, suggesting that Aschenbach created them. His novel *Königliche Hoheit* (Royal Highness, 1909) revolves around the issue of *Repräsentation*, of playing a public role.

Its main figure is an imaginary prince, but his public duties and private isolation are related to those of artists. Aschenbach, too, plays such a role, as Mann indicates by using the verb *repräsentieren* in connection with his career. In chapter 2 of *Death in Venice*, he also alludes to this prince, again as one of Aschenbach's creations. Furthermore, Mann says Aschenbach once wrote that nearly everything great exists as a *Trotzdem* (Despite). Mann himself wrote this in *Über den Alkohol* (On Alcohol, 1906). He mentions four unfinished literary efforts, too. The list of Aschenbach's works given at the beginning of chapter 2 cites a prose epic about the life of Frederick the Great (1712–86), a novel named *Maya*, a story titled *Ein Elender* (An Outcast), and the essay *Geist und Kunst* (Intellect and Art). Mann himself planned but then never wrote these works. Instead of an entire novel about Frederick the Great, he wrote the essay *Friedrich und die große Koalition* (Frederick and the Grand Coalition, 1915). This essay draws parallels between the First World War and the military and diplomatic skill of that Prussian king. Mann implies that Aschenbach was ennobled—dubbed Gustav *von* Aschenbach—because of his biographical epos about Frederick. It thus seems likely that Aschenbach, too, has written something rather patriotic. Mann incorporated material originally destined for *Maya* into *Doktor Faustus*, moreover, and his ideas about the relationship of intellect to art inform this novel as well as many of his essays. By attributing these works to Aschenbach, who *has* finished them, Mann is apparently freeing himself from the difficulties they caused. He also seems to resolve such problems more easily than Aschenbach, whose acute case of writer's block at the outset of *Death in Venice* proves fatal. This scapegoating or loading of one's own failed projects onto one's protagonist, who is then sent to his death, suggests how complex Mann's autobiographical allusions can be. He and Aschenbach often appear similar—and, to a limited extent, they do resemble each other—but they are hardly identical.

Even more revealing and detailed comparisons can be drawn between *Death in Venice* and four of Mann's earlier novellas. Despite his name, which contains the noun *Friede* (peace), the title character of *Der kleine Herr Friedemann* has his peace of mind shattered and commits suicide. This catastrophe is the culmination of a life marked by unfortunate events. When he is a month old, a drunken nurse lets him fall from a table. He survives a slight concussion but grows up misshapen. When he is seven, he goes to school but cannot play with the other children. As a result, he has no camaraderie with them. At sixteen, he falls in love with a girl whom he then sees kissing another boy. He decides not to bother with this sort of thing ever again. It may afford others happiness and joy, he thinks, but to him it can bring only grief and sorrow. He thus renounces all romantic interests, and he pursues aesthetic pleasures instead. He loves life and enjoys it. He especially loves music, and he cultivates his literary taste. He is also receptive to all his feelings and moods, including his unfulfilled wishes, his yearning. At thirty, he expects to live another ten or twenty years, which he awaits in peace. Then, during a performance of *Lohengrin* (1850), an opera by Richard Wagner, he sits next to Gerda von Rinnlingen, the enigmatic wife of a military officer. Friedemann turns pale and perspires. His heart pounds, and he leaves. He also whispers her name as he leans against a lamppost, and poetry runs through his head as he falls into a feverish sleep. Gerda has reawakened all that he has suppressed. Later, at a party given by the Rinnlingens, he wears red stockings and watches her from a distance. They then take a walk in the garden and sit on a bench at the edge of the river. She asks if he has been unhappy all his life and says she understands unhappiness. He kneels before her and tries to say what he feels, but she grabs him by the arm, throws him to the ground, and gets up and walks away. Friedemann, beside himself, crawls into the water and drowns. *Death in Venice* recalls this novella in several ways. Aschenbach, too, has a symbolic name. It contains the word *Asche* (ash), which hints that he is burned out, emotionally exhausted. His doctors prevent him from attending school, so he, like Friedemann, grows up without comrades. He eventually reacts to Tadzio, the boy he silently admires in Venice, much as Friedemann reacts to Gerda. He sweats, his heart pounds, he leans against the door of Tadzio's room, and he publicly whispers, "I love you." Poetry runs through his head as well, he becomes feverish, and he ultimately wears something red. He also watches Tadzio from afar and, perhaps willingly, goes to his death near water. On a more general level, these parallels hint that *Death in Venice*, too, is about the eruption of suppressed desire.

A second novella that Mann wrote prior to *Death in Venice* and that helps explain Aschenbach's adventures is *Gladius Dei*. Its title means "sword of God" and comes from a book by Savonarola, the monk who was the model for one of the two main characters in Mann's *Fiorenza*.[2] Like that play, this second earlier novella opposes religious morals to aesthetic enjoyment. It is set in Munich, a city that it famously describes as art-loving and easygoing. Young people there whistle a motif—a significant series of notes—from Wagner's opera *Der Ring des Nibelungen* (The Ring of the Nibelungs, 1876). Artists pay their rent with their sketches, moreover, and ogle the local women, whose morals are not terribly strict. In this artsy metropolis, beauty is a source of pleasure and profit. In the window of an art gallery, Hieronymus, a young man who looks and acts like Savonarola, sees a photograph of a model posing as the Madonna. She is very feminine, and the child she is holding as if it were Jesus is playing with her naked breast and casting a suggestive glance. Two other, less pious young men say that the child looks as if it means to make one envious and that the sensuous model makes one doubt the doctrine of Immaculate Conception. Hieronymus hears them and goes home, where no amount of prayer gets this Madonna out of his mind. A voice from on high then commands him to speak out against wicked ideas of beauty. The weather is sultry, and a storm threatens. He returns to the gallery and demands that the erotic photograph be removed, even burned. It is a product as well as an object of sensual lust, he argues, and calling it beauty is simply unconscionable. Knowledge is torture but necessary to one's salvation, he insists, and art should be a holy torch that illuminates the terrible abysses of human existence. The employees laugh at him, and the owner has him thrown out. Madly and ecstatically, Hieronymus then envisions the art in the gallery being consumed by flames. He also envisions a flaming sword, which he calls down upon the sinful earth. *Death in Venice* is like *Gladius Dei* in several respects. Aschenbach journeys south from Munich. He has chosen to reside in this artistic capital, so his attraction to Tadzio's beauty is neither sudden nor surprising. Furthermore, his aestheticism, his appreciation of beauty, is counterbalanced by his asceticism, his austere self-discipline. Hieronymus is similarly monkish, but his struggle to dispel his image of the seductive Madonna hints that asceticism may result from suppressed desires. When Hieronymus speaks in favor of knowledge, moreover, he rejects *Unbefangenheit* (ingenuousness, naiveté). Aschenbach does the opposite: he regains naiveté by rejecting knowledge. Finally, as in the last scene of *Gladius Dei*, it is sultry and stormy in the first one of *Death in Venice*. In both of these scenes, the hero has a vision, and Mann introduces each vision with the same repeated phrase: "Er sah . . . Er sah" (He saw . . . He saw). These similarities suggest that *Death in Venice*, too, is a novella about the sensual nature of beauty and the uncertain morality of aestheticism.

Comparisons can also be drawn between *Death in Venice* and a third novella that Mann had already written. As its title implies, *Tristan* alludes to Wagner's opera *Tristan und Isolde* (1865). It does so in a way reminiscent of references to Wagner in *Der kleine Herr Friedemann* and *Gladius Dei*. As noted above, Johannes Friedemann is smitten by Gerda von Rinnlingen at a performance of Wagner's *Lohengrin*, and young people in

Munich whistle a motif from *Der Ring des Nibelungen*. This motif, like the title of *Gladius Dei*, refers to a sword. The turning point of *Tristan* likewise involves the performance of Wagner's music, which its characters similarly reproduce. The novella also reworks the emotional triangle in which Wagner's main medieval characters are caught. It is set in a sanatorium called "Einfried," a name like that of Wagner's villa, "Wahnfried." Like the name "Friedemann," moreover, *Einfried* suggests *Friede* (peace) that is destroyed. The patients include Detlev Spinell, a writer similar to Aschenbach, though he is also a caricature. His hair, too, is graying at the temples. He, too, gets up early and washes in cold water, practicing such strict habits because his literary profession gives him a bad conscience. He, too, writes slowly, creating an appearance of smoothness and vivacity. Spinell also goes to ridiculous extremes. His aestheticism, his worship of beauty, is so exaggerated that it is ludicrous. He also derives composure and dignity from the style of the furniture at the sanatorium. Mann casts further doubt on him by using quotation marks to tell how he "worked." Finally, Spinell prefers the beauty of death to the ugliness of life. He thus embodies an idea expressed in a poem by August von Platen (1796–1835). That poem—it, too, is entitled "Tristan"—says that whoever sees beauty is consigned to death, useless in life, and eternally in love. Another patient, Gabriele Klöterjahn, is a victim of this romantic and decadent thought. She is a delicate young wife and mother, and she has been ill since the birth of her robust son. Her husband is a crass, successful businessman. Spinell's compliments make her feverish, and at his urging she disobeys her doctors by playing piano excerpts from *Tristan und Isolde*. Her health then declines and she dies of tuberculosis. In a comic confrontation, her husband has berated Spinell for writing to him about his, Klöterjahn's, supposed lack of awareness. Mann pokes fun at both the precious Spinell and the philistine Klöterjahn. *Tristan* thus displays some of the themes of *Death in Venice* in a humorous and critical light. It makes an author rather like Aschenbach seem foolish and dangerous. It also travesties enthusiasm for Wagner, who wrote part of *Tristan und Isolde* in Venice, where he died. It mocks the notion that being drawn to death is aesthetic, a result of fascination with beauty. This notion comes from Platen, to whom Mann alludes as Aschenbach approaches Venice. *Tristan* links disease and decadence as well. Not only is Gabriele too fine for her vigorous husband and their son; Spinell's teeth are unhealthy, too. In *Death in Venice*, so are Tadzio's. Finally, when Mann opposes Spinell to Klöterjahn, his irony and ambivalence are plain. He distances himself from both these characters, wavering between the artistic and bourgeois values they respectively represent. *Death in Venice* contrasts these same values. It does so more solemnly, but it, too, is often composed in an ironic and intentionally ambiguous style.

Another of Mann's novellas that help understand *Death in Venice* is *Tonio Kröger*. Its title character is an author faced with the same literary-artistic crisis that confronted Aschenbach before the events of *Death in Venice* begin. *Tonio Kröger* describes this crisis more clearly than the later novella, and its hero deals with it differently. The crisis has to do with knowledge, with a writer's psychological insights, and it occurs at a turning point in Tonio Kröger's life. When he was fourteen, he had a crush on blond Hans Hansen, a fellow schoolboy. At sixteen, he loved an equally blonde girl, Ingeborg Holm. Now in his early thirties, he is successful but troubled. As he explains to a Russian painter, art alienates artists from humanity. To tastefully present human emotion, he argues, they have to be cold and distanced. An artist therefore cannot be human. Tonio Kröger has already learned that good works of art arise from an awful life and that whoever lives cannot create. He adds that life is the opposite of art and intellect, and he yearns for it, for the bliss of human normalcy. He praises such bliss on a trip to Denmark, where he vacations after visiting his birthplace in northern Germany and where he encounters a couple like Hans and Ingeborg. Writing to his Russian friend, he acknowledges that he is a bourgeois Bohemian, an artist with a bad conscience. His bourgeois love of normal human life, he also observes, is the saving grace of his art. Many details of this novella recur in *Death in Venice*, a fact that lends them special significance. Most of them show how Tonio Kröger resembles Aschenbach. Tonio Kröger, too, lives in Munich and has trouble writing in the spring, which he says is a difficult time of year because it makes one feel. His work, too, has exhausted him. In fact, Mann mentions the "Asche seiner Müdigkeit" (the ash of his fatigue), a phrase that helps grasp Aschenbach's name. As noted above, it contains the word *Asche* (ash), which here clearly connotes fatigue. Like Aschenbach, Tonio Kröger loves the sea, arrives at a fancy hotel on foot, has odd dreams, and grooms himself meticulously. There is a tiger on the ship that carries him to Denmark, just as there is one in Aschenbach's vision of a tropical landscape. Both of these characters watch the sunrise on a day that is a high point of their yearning, and in both their stories Mann describes waves as charging steers. Both lose track of how long they have been on vacation. Just as Aschenbach tries but fails to exchange a few words with Tadzio, moreover, Tonio Kröger considers chatting with the couple like Hans and Ingeborg but lacks the courage to do so. More generally, Tonio Kröger, too, is an artist skeptical of art. He, too, dresses well while leading an adventurous inner life, sharing his ancestors' suspicion of artists. His mother, even more clearly than Aschenbach's, is southern and musical. Finally, he, too, has an affinity for the author Friedrich Schiller (1759–1805). Mann says that serious readers likened Aschenbach's *Geist und Kunst* to Schiller's *Über naive und sentimentalische Dichtung* (On Naive and Sentimental Poetry, 1795–96). Young Tonio tells Hans about Schiller's play *Don Carlos* (1787). For that matter, Hans, like Tadzio, is blond and wears a sailor suit. The presence of these many details in both novellas suggests that Aschenbach may share Tonio Kröger's larger problems.

Death in Venice does indeed mention the main issue that troubles Tonio Kröger: the issue of knowledge. It does so only briefly, though, almost in passing. In his second chapter, Mann notes that Aschenbach once overworked knowledge, which can quickly lose its charm. Aschenbach's story *Ein Elender*, moreover, shows readers the possibility of moral resolve beyond the most profound knowledge. This resolve has to do with his rejection of indecent psychologism, a concept that suggests moral laxity and relativism. Aschenbach himself later imagines Plato's Socrates saying that writers reject knowledge because it is the abyss. Mann also hints that going beyond what one knows is ethically dubious. *Death in Venice* appears to prove this point insofar as Aschenbach ignores his feelings and then conducts himself incorrectly. Mann does not clarify these statements about knowledge, though, and they often seem cryptic. In *Gladius Dei*, as noted above, the heated Hieronymus says that knowledge is torture but necessary to one's salvation. He also implies that art should provide it. These remarks, too, seem weighty yet vague. *Tonio Kröger* raises the issue of knowledge more clearly and in greater detail. As a boy, its hero finds psychological insights into human nature more important and interesting than the kind of knowledge taught in school. He sees through his teachers' foibles, and he knows that not everyone looks into things deeply, to the point where things become complicated and sad. He sees through empty words and deeds, sees into human souls, but what he finds is farce and misery. With such knowledge of people comes isolation from them. Knowledge of the human soul would make one gloomy, he also says, were it not for the pleasures afforded by literary form and expression. To his Russian friend, he claims that such pleasures are not always sufficient compensation for psychological insight into the sadness of the world. Knowledge, he explains, can fill one with disgust. This is the case with Hamlet, whose Danish home he subsequently visits. Knowledge is old and boring, he adds, and literature, which provides it, makes one tired. He longs to be free of the curse of knowledge even near the end of his story, but by then he can also recall how it formerly made him desolate and paralyzed. Since he embraces a bourgeois love of humanity, as noted above, it no longer does. He thereby has overcome the same artistic crisis that destroys Aschenbach. Despite all the similarities between their stories, these heroes accordingly differ. When he sees his Russian friend, Tonio Kröger wonders if he should have gone for a walk instead, though he doubts that doing so would have made him feel any better. Aschenbach takes just such a walk, and it turns out to be the beginning of the end for him. Like Aschenbach, Tonio Kröger has also been to Italy. He there engaged in adventures of the flesh. His senses disgusted him and he hated them, but he was torn between the extremes of icy intellectualism and consuming sensuality. Now he rejects the idea of traveling to Italy. The thought of all that *bellezza*, its beauty, makes him nervous. As a result, he journeys north to Copenhagen, not south to Venice. Nonetheless, the fact that Mann addresses the problem of knowledge again in *Death in Venice* hints that his answer to it in *Tonio Kröger* was only temporary and too optimistic.

DEATH IN VENICE AND WORLD LITERATURE

Mann's novella bears similarities not only to his other writings but also to works by other authors. Some of these works will be mentioned below, in chapter 4, as literary influences. Others will likewise be cited later, in chapter 5, to help explain Mann's ideas. Some of them are from ancient Greece; others are from modern Germany. They include Homer's *Odyssey*, to which Mann alludes when he suggests how Aschenbach loves and dies. They also include Euripides' *Bacchae*, a tragedy whose title betrays that it is about female followers of the god Dionysus, or Bacchus. This is the "foreign god" worshiped in Aschenbach's orgiastic dream. Other ancient texts that are related to *Death in Venice* and discussed below are Plato's *Phaedrus* and *Symposium*, Xenophon's *Memorabilia*, and Plutarch's *Erotikos*. These four texts resemble Mann's story, since they, too, discuss lust, love, and the elevating force of beauty. One might also mention the Roman poet Virgil (70 B.C.E.–19 C.E.), whom Mann quotes in the working notes he made for his novella and whose second eclogue has been likened to it.[3] This bucolic poem, like that novella, addresses the issue of homosexual love. Modern German literary works like *Death in Venice*, as noted below, include Goethe's *Die Wahlverwandtschaften* (Elective Affinities, 1809), a novel whose title is a scientific term suggesting its fateful tale of its characters' erotic attractions. Like this novel, Goethe's story *Der Mann von funfzig Jahren* (A Man of Fifty), told in his subsequent *Wilhelm Meisters Wanderjahre* (Wilhelm Meister's Journeyman Years, 1821–29), is about an aging man in love. This topic recurs not only in *Death in Venice* but also in Goethe's *Faust* (1808–32). Goethe's description of Faust's sensual journey during Walpurgis Night (30 April), moreover, resembles Mann's account of Aschenbach's sultry dream. Mann's novella addresses problems of artistic consciousness, moral grace and dignity, and aesthetic education, too, problems raised in aesthetic essays by Friedrich Schiller discussed below. It also addresses related issues raised in a similar essay, one on marionettes, by Heinrich von Kleist (1777–1811). This essay is likewise treated below. So are sonnets by August von Platen that were inspired, in Venice, by some of the same sights and emotions that Aschenbach sees and feels. Furthermore, Mann's novella recalls both the enthusiastic neoclassicism of Friedrich Hölderlin (1770–1843) and the morbid aestheticism of Stefan George (1868–1933). Finally, in name and in kind, Mann's hero is very like Gustave Flaubert (1821–90).

Death in Venice is also like other fiction written prior to it. In theme or style, for example, it resembles seven novels or stories that preceded it in the last decade of the nineteenth century or the first few years of the twentieth. Oscar Wilde's *The Picture of Dorian Gray* (1891), too, seems to condemn amoral aestheticism, an ethically neutral devotion to beauty. Like Mann, Wilde links this artistic attitude with homoeroticism, the sexual longing of one male for another. Joseph Conrad's *Heart of Darkness* (1899) employs exoticism, a fascination with a foreign country or culture, in much the same way that *Death in Venice* does, namely to recount a trip to the inner reaches of human nature. Like Mann, Conrad describes horrific urges that lie just beneath the veneer of European civilization. Gabriele D'Annunzio's *Il fuoco* (The Flame, 1900) takes place in Venice, which it, like *Death in Venice*, describes as the site of fading power and beauty. In this sense, the famous city, in both works, seems decadent. D'Annunzio's hero is a poet who admires Wagner, moreover, and lives according to certain ideas of Nietzsche. This same operatic composer and this same philosopher figure in Mann's novella, though it does not mention them by name. André Gide's *L'immoraliste* (The Immoralist, 1902) likewise shows the influence of Nietzsche, not to mention the exoticism of Africa again. Its studious hero, like Aschenbach, discovers sensual urges and homosexual leanings as he ever more questionably defies puritanic conventions. Henry James's *The Beast in the Jungle* (1903) is like *Death in*

Venice insofar as its hero's inkling of his fate, his failure to live passion-ately, is symbolized by a crouching tiger. Like Aschenbach, James's hero envisions this symbol in a hallucination at a cemetery. *Death in Venice* also resembles Heinrich Mann's *Die Göttinnen* (The Goddesses, 1902). This novel, too, is about exaggerated aestheticism and decadence, topics that it treats under the influence of Nietzsche and Greek mythology. Like Aschenbach, Heinrich's heroine sojourns in Venice and suffers from wan-ing vitality.[4] Finally, parallels can be drawn between *Death in Venice* and Heinrich's *Professor Unrat* (1905), the source of the film *The Blue Angel* (1930). Heinrich's title character is a tyrannical high school teacher. Like Aschenbach, he discovers his repressed sensuality in a manner that undermines his stature as a representative of bourgeois culture under Wilhelm II, the emperor who ruled Germany from 1888 to 1918.[5] Like many of these other and prior works of fiction, *Death in Venice* contains autobiographical elements, episodes that actually happened in the life of its author, and it combines realistic and symbolic narrative styles. After one reads these works alongside *Death in Venice*, moreover, one appreci-ates, among other things, just how gently it hints at its intellectual influ-ences and at its political import.

Mann's novella may also be compared to seven works of fiction writ-ten after it. These works, like those written before it, often differ from it, but they are nonetheless similar, sometimes in revealing ways. James Joyce's *A Portrait of the Artist as a Young Man* (1914-15), too, is a partly autobiographical novel about the evolution of an artist. Aschenbach is no longer young, of course, but *Death in Venice* might well be called a por-trait of the artist as an old, or at least as a middle-aged, man. What is more, both works contain many passages that reflect the consciousness of their respective protagonists. Hermann Broch's *Der Tod des Vergil* (The Death of Virgil, 1945) is another novel that conveys the consciousness of a lit-erary artist. Like *Death in Venice*, it calls literary art into question and casts doubt on the aesthetic attitude. Its Virgil, like Aschenbach, is dying and is led in his last hours by a boy who plays the role of Hermes, a Greek god who conducted souls to the underworld.[6] Yukio Mishima's *Kinjiki* (For-bidden Colors, 1951-53) tells of another famous, aging author who, like Aschenbach, is attracted to a handsome young man at the beach. This author, in postwar Japan, hates psychology, has trouble writing, and re-calls Plato's *Phaedrus* and *Symposium*, just as Aschenbach does. Mishima's story, like Mann's, also asks larger questions about art, beauty, and death. Wolfgang Koeppen's *Der Tod in Rom* (Death in Rome, 1954) alludes to Mann's tale in both its title and its final line. That line reports the death of a former Nazi general in Rome. His nephew is an avant-garde composer whose homosexual tryst with a boy prostitute is a far cry from Aschenbach's relatively restrained admiration of Tadzio. Koeppen thus seems to mock Mann. Vladimir Nabokov's *Lolita* (1955) again recalls Mann's novella. It, too, tells of a man who desires an adolescent, though the young person is a "nymphet," the hero's knowing and attractive step-daughter. In contrast with this hero, Aschenbach keeps his desire under control and does not commit any statutory crimes.[7] Max Frisch's *Homo Faber* (1957) is likewise about sexual love that a man feels for his daughter. As its title implies, this man is a technologist, a man who makes machines and does not believe in irrational forces or fate. Like Aschenbach, he succumbs to just such forces and to a fate that is occasioned by ignoring his emotions. Elements of human nature embodied in Greek myths catch up with him, too. Finally, Ian McEwan's *The Comfort of Strangers* (1981), like much recent fiction that seems to echo Mann's story, is set in a Venice that is the confusing site of a fatal, erotic stalking. Like many of these other and later works of fiction, *Death in Venice* often draws on its author's experiences and describes fictional events from its hero's subjective point of view. What one notices most when one reads them together with it, however, is that Mann raises issues they have in common, particularly the issues of pedophilia and homoeroticism, with comparative delicacy and discretion. In fact, understanding its significance, alone as well as in the larger context of world literature, often requires appreciating its subtlety.

NOTES

1. *Death in Venice and Other Stories*, trans. David Luke (New York: Bantam, 1988); *Death in Venice and Other Tales*, trans. Joachim Neugroschel (New York: Viking Penguin, 1998).

2. The book is Savonarola's *Compendium Revelationum* (1495). According to Hans Rudolf Vaget, Mann found the quotation containing the phrase "Gladius Dei" in a nineteenth-century biography of Savonarola. See Hans Rudolf Vaget, *Thomas Mann: Kommentar zu sämtlichen Erzählungen* (Munich: Winkler, 1984), 100.

3. See Ernst A. Schmidt, "Künstler und Knabenliebe: Eine vergleichende Skizze zu Thomas Manns *Tod in Venedig* und Vergils zweiter Ekloge," *Euphorion* 68.4 (1974): 437–46.

4. See Renate Werner, *Skeptizismus, Ästhetizismus, Aktivismus: Der frühe Heinrich Mann* (Düsseldorf: Bertelsmann, 1972), 117–44.

5. See Walter H. Sokel, "Demaskierung und Untergang wilhelminischer Repräsentanz: Zum Parallelismus der Inhaltsstruktur von *Professor Unrat* und 'Tod

in Venedig,'" in *Herkommen und Erneuerung: Essays für Oskar Seidlin*, ed. Gerald Gillespie and Edgar Lohner (Tübingen: Niemeyer, 1976), 387–412.

6. See Doris Stephan, "Thomas Mann's 'Tod in Venedig' und Brochs 'Vergil,'" *Schweizer Monatshefte* 40.1 (April 1960): 76–83.

7. See Margaret Morganroth Gullette, "The Exile of Adulthood: Pedophilia in the Midlife Novel," *Novel* 17.3 (Spring 1984): 215–32.

2   Content

The fictional events recounted in *Death in Venice* take place over the course of about two months. Its principal character, Gustav von Aschenbach, first takes a walk in Munich at the beginning of May. Roughly two weeks later, he leaves for an unnamed island in the Adriatic Sea. A week and a half after arriving on that island, he decides to go to Venice instead, where he falls in love with Tadzio, a beautiful Polish boy. In the fourth week of his stay there, Aschenbach starts to notice that something is wrong in the world around him, and he soon learns that the city has been stricken with a cholera epidemic. Several days later, he dies after eating overripe strawberries and collapsing at the beach on the Lido, a barrier island between the Adriatic and the Venetian lagoon. This sequence of events occurs in ways and for reasons more complex than a mere summary of Mann's plot can convey. Indeed, *what* happens in his story is often far less interesting and less important than *how* it happens and *why* it happens. As the second of his five chapters shows, one also must know *to whom* it happens. Nothing at all, in fact, happens in that second chapter. The plot stands still, and one could jump from the end of chapter 1 to the beginning of chapter 3 without missing any of the external action. One could read the last sentence of chapter 1, that is, and the first sentence of chapter 3 as if they were run together without interruption. The sentence from chapter 1 tells how Aschenbach loses sight of a wanderer he sees at a cemetery in Munich; the one from chapter 3 tells how he delays carrying out his decision to travel south: "But the man's whereabouts were not clear to Aschenbach, since he was to be found neither in his previous location, nor elsewhere at the streetcar stop, nor in the streetcar itself. . . . Several matters of worldly and literary nature detained Aschenbach, who was eager to travel, for about two more weeks after that walk in Munich." As in much great fiction, however, it is precisely when nothing happens that the most important things get said. Mann begins in *medias res*, in the middle of his story, without any preliminary remarks. Only after relating the episode described in chapter 1 does he mention, in chapter 2, the events that preceded it, only then telling how Aschenbach had lived and worked before that fateful day in May. It is Aschenbach's strict way of life and his work habits, moreover, his psychological profile and artistic career, which lead to the events of *Death in Venice* and lend them meaning. Those events themselves occur on only the most obvious and superficial level of a rich and complex text. In other words, Mann's plot is only part of his story.

CHAPTER 1

The first chapter of *Death in Venice* is set in Munich at the beginning of May in a year given only as "19. . ." It introduces Mann's main character, the author Gustav von Aschenbach, and it describes what Aschenbach sees while on a walk he takes one afternoon. Some of what he sees actually exists within the fictional world of Mann's story, some of it is imagined by Aschenbach alone, and some of it could be either actual or imaginary, either objectively part of that fictional world or the product of Aschenbach's subjective vision. Furthermore, some of what he sees existed in the Munich where Mann himself lived when he wrote the novella in 1911 and 1912. There are thus four modes of reality in chapter 1. The first three are fictional, and *Death in Venice* mixes and moves among them in ways showing, or at least suggesting, that much of what it relates is not only narrated from Aschenbach's point of view but also exists solely in his tired and troubled mind. The fourth is historical, and it hints at Mann's own life and at links between him and his protagonist. His subtle combination of these four modes of reality, like the fact that his plot is not the whole story he tells, makes it seem naive to read *Death in Venice* as if it were purely naturalistic, as if it merely imitated or reproduced external events.

Chapter 1 begins by stating Aschenbach's name, hinting at his age, alluding to when his story takes place, mentioning his address, and saying he has gone for a walk. He is Gustav *von* Aschenbach, having been ennobled on his fiftieth birthday, and it is the spring of a year in which

Europe has somehow been threatened. Aschenbach lives on Prinzregent-enstraße (Prince Regent Street), an address that connotes high social rank and significant wealth. He has set out on his walk alone. Enervated by the difficult and dangerous writing he did that morning, he was unable to stop the internal mechanism of his eloquence and unable to sleep, as he must once a day, now that his strength has started to wane. He went out after tea, hoping that motion and fresh air would revive him.

Mann next talks about the weather. (For remarks on the distinction between Mann and his narrator, see chapter 6.) It is the beginning of May, but a false high summer has set in, and the English Garden, a large public park in Munich, is as sultry as in August. Walking at first through that park and then outside of it, Aschenbach is described as being increasingly far from other people. Because he is tired and a storm is brewing, he waits for a streetcar at the North Cemetery. A shift in the tense of Mann's verbs at this point indicates that we have reached the present time of his story and that the events of *Death in Venice* start, strictly speaking, with Aschenbach's waiting for the streetcar.

Aschenbach's surroundings are now described in detail. His streetcar stop is deserted, and so are the stonemasons' shops nearby, where crosses, gravestones, and funerary monuments are for sale. Aschenbach spends several minutes reading and contemplating the liturgical sayings about life after death inscribed on a mortuary chapel across the street. This chapel is said to be "Byzantine," that is, in the architectural style of the eastern part of the later Roman Empire. Aschenbach awakens from his reveries and notices a man standing in its portico. Statues of two apocalyptic animals guard the steps leading to that porch, which suggests that this scene foretells violent events. The man's appearance makes Aschenbach's thoughts take a different turn.

That appearance is striking and strange. Among other things, the man has a pug nose and red hair. He does not look Bavarian—as might be expected, since the scene is set in Munich, the capital of Bavaria—and his straw hat gives him an air of foreignness. He leans on his walking stick and stands with his feet crossed. His Adam's apple stands out, and with energetic furrows between his eyebrows, he gazes into the distance. His pose seems imperious, bold, and even wild. His lips seem too short, for they reveal his long white teeth.

This strange man returns Aschenbach's stare so aggressively that Aschenbach turns away and decides not to pay attention to him. He quickly forgets him, but he is soon conscious of an expansive feeling, a feeling of unrest, a youthful desire to travel.

This feeling is so powerful and passionate that Aschenbach has a vision. Mann writes, "Seine Begierde ward sehend" (His desire became seeing), and Aschenbach imagines or "sees" a tropical landscape. This swamp contains luxuriant plants and exotic animals, including palm trees whose trunks are hairy and tigers whose eyes sparkle. This vision fills Aschenbach's heart with horror as well as longing. When it fades, he paces near the masons' gravestones.

Aschenbach's attitude toward travel reflects his strict work ethic. He regards travel as nothing other than a hygienic measure, one that must be taken, reluctantly, now and then. Too busy with tasks set by his ego and the European soul, he has not traveled far and has never been tempted to leave Europe. Since his life has started to wane and he has feared not being able to finish his work, he has confined himself to Munich and to his summer home in the mountains.

In this case, however, he decides to take a break. At first, his reason and self-discipline temper his desire to travel. He does not want a trip to interrupt his work. Aschenbach admits, though, that he wants to get away from that work. Although he almost enjoys the daily battle between his will and fatigue, it seems best not to stifle such a pressing need. The thought of the difficulty he is having with his writing fills him with disgust. He is paralyzed by his scruples, by an insatiable perfectionism. He regards perfectionism as the essence of talent and has curbed his feelings for its sake. Are those feelings now taking their revenge by refusing to inspire his art? Mann asks this question in a way implying that it could be occurring to Aschenbach himself. (For remarks on the concept of free indirect discourse, see chapter 6.) The nation honors Aschenbach's mastery, but Aschenbach thinks that his work lacks verve. He fears spending the summer at his house in the mountains, and he decides to travel, to take a siesta of three or four weeks somewhere in the south.

The chapter ends as Aschenbach gets into the streetcar and decides to spend the evening studying maps and train schedules. He looks for but cannot find the man who prompted this episode.

CHAPTER 2

Mann's second chapter provides the biographical background that makes his hero's story significant. This chapter tells about Aschenbach's writings, family, youth, and fame. It also mentions the extreme effort that his writing takes, and it explains his rapport with his readers, the traits of his own fictional heroes, the course of his career, and his literary style. Finally, it describes his physical appearance. These aspects of his work, life, and person are revealed in a portrait of an artist whose current fatigue and future actions seem to result largely from his past.

The chapter opens with a sentence that lists Aschenbach's writings before it says anything about his life. Those writings include an epic about Frederick the Great (1712–86), a famous king of Prussia; the novel *Maja*; the story *Ein Elender* (An Outcast); and the treatise *Geist und Kunst* (Intellect and Art). Aschenbach was born in the city of "L" in Silesia, a province that now lies mostly in Poland. His ancestors were officers, judges, and civil servants. His mother, the daughter of a Bohemian bandleader, brought faster and more sensual blood, as Mann puts it, into the family. His inherited combination of sober conscientiousness and darker, more fiery impulses produced the artist that he is.

Aschenbach wanted fame, and he achieved it early. He made a name for himself while he was almost still in high school. Later he had to play a public role and manage his fame. By the age of forty, fatigued from his work, he had to answer letters from all over the world.

Aschenbach's talent, which was neither banal nor eccentric, appealed both to a broad audience and to more particular readers. Driven to achieve, he never knew the idleness of youth. When he fell ill at thirty-five, an astute observer said that he had always lived like a clenched fist. Hardly robust, he was called but not born to such constant tension.

Aschenbach made a virtue of his physical frailty. Too weak to go to school, he grew up without friends and soon learned that talented people like him seldom lived long. His favorite word was *Durchhalten* (Persevere), however, and he wished to grow old so that he could be fruitful, as an artist, at all stages of life.

Accordingly, he needed the discipline that he luckily inherited from his father's side of the family. After splashing cold water on himself, for example, he spent two or three hours writing every morning. That readers took his prose, which he thus wrote piecemeal, for the product of single, longer sittings indicated the triumph of his stern morality. As an artist, Aschenbach thus displayed endurance and toughness like the kind shown by Frederick the Great when he conquered Silesia in the 1740s.

Aschenbach once said that everything great exists as a *Trotzdem* (Despite), that is, despite emotional, material, physical, and moral obstacles and difficulties. He knew that this was true from experience, and it was the formula for his life and the key to his art. It also occurred in his fictional characters.

The kind of fictional heroes he preferred all displayed what a critic had called an intellectual and youthful manliness that proudly and calmly endures swords and spears piercing its body. Mann notes that Saint

Sebastian, a Christian martyr who was killed in a similar way, is a perfect symbol of Aschenbach's art. In Aschenbach's fictional world, he explains, one sees such elegant self-control as well as other examples of a heroism of weakness. What heroism, he asks, would be more appropriate for Aschenbach's times? Aschenbach speaks for all who work on the verge of exhaustion, for all these moralists of achievement. They are the heroes of the age, and they recognize themselves in his works, which they grate-fully praise. Mann thus explains Aschenbach's success as the result of sym-pathy between him and his contemporaries.

Aschenbach was in tune with his times earlier, too. In his youth he was coarse, as they were. He made mistakes and gave offense. He achieved dignity, though, and one can say, Mann writes, that his entire develop-ment was an ascent to dignity, a rise that transcended doubt and irony.

Among his mistakes as a problematic young man was his cynical atti-tude toward art and artists. He conveyed that attitude to other, like-minded young people even as he delighted the gullible bourgeois masses with his tangible literary images.

To people like Aschenbach, however, Mann goes on to say, knowledge quickly loses its charm. Youthful thoroughness seems shallow, he adds, compared to a mature man's decision to deny knowledge insofar as it hin-ders will, deeds, feelings, or passion. Aschenbach's *Ein Elender* reveals disgust with the indecent psychologism of his day. That story proclaims aversion to moral skepticism, to sympathy with the abyss. It also rejects the laxity of the compassionate maxim that to understand is to forgive. It thereby indicates a "Wunder der wiedergeborenen Unbefangenheit" (miracle of reborn naiveté). Was it a result of this "renaissance" that Aschenbach's sense of beauty seemed to grow stronger? Does moral reso-lution beyond knowledge not imply an ethical simplification and thereby encourage what is evil and forbidden? And is form not moral and amoral alike, even immoral? Aschenbach's evolution as an artist thus raises seri-ous ethical and aesthetic questions. In this chapter, those questions seem to come directly from Mann.

Such questions did not impede Aschenbach's public career. In time, there was something official and pedagogical about his works. His style became more polished and traditional, more formal and elevated. Selec-tions from his works became required reading in schools. At the age of fifty, he was ennobled by a German prince.

Aschenbach chose Munich as his permanent residence. Although an intellectual, he led a life of bourgeois respectability. His wife died soon after their marriage. He had a married daughter, but he never possessed a son.

The chapter ends with a description of Aschenbach's appearance. His head and face reveal his age and reflect stress caused by his artistic career. Personally, too, Mann writes, art is a heightened life. It delights more deeply and consumes more quickly. It engraves one's face and stimulates one's nerves. With such general remarks on art and artists, Mann indicates that Aschenbach's story is only one instance of broader issues.

CHAPTER 3

The third chapter of *Death in Venice* begins with Aschenbach's departure from Munich and ends with his decision not to leave Venice. It is thus a transition between the exposition of the novella and its high point and dénouement. Using such terms to talk about Mann's story, as if it were a play, makes sense because that story unfolds in dramatic fashion. The conflict and the emotions that it treats become clearer here, and Aschenbach's actions sometimes seem tragic. Is he a victim of fate? Will he be a hero? Chapter 3 invites such questions by introducing Tadzio, Mann's other main character, as well as several minor characters who have important roles. In this chapter, then, Mann's plot thickens.

The chapter starts by relating the initial stages of Aschenbach's trip. He remains in Munich for about two weeks after his walk and orders his summerhouse to be ready for him within a further four. One day between the middle and end of May, he takes the train to Trieste, where he spends twenty-four hours before going on to Pola. At the time when the story takes place, both these cities were part of the Austro-Hungarian Empire.

Aschenbach does not stay long at his first vacation spot. He wants something foreign but not far away, so he goes to an island off the coast of Istria, a peninsula in present-day Croatia. The weather is bad, though, he does not like the other, Austrian guests at his hotel, and he cannot establish a contemplative relationship with the sea. About ten days after arriving, he therefore returns to Pola and is en route to Venice.

The dingy boat that Aschenbach takes has a suspiciously courteous crew. He buys a ticket from a man who looks like an old-fashioned circus director and who is quick to praise the many attractions of Venice.

Before the boat departs, Aschenbach regards people on the dock as well as his fellow passengers. Among the latter is a boisterous group of young clerks from Pola. Aschenbach is horrified when he realizes that one of them is false, or old. This older man is wearing a yellow suit, a red tie, and a panama hat. He also wears makeup, a wig, and dentures. Aschenbach wonders whether the young men know he is old and why they tolerate him. It seems to Aschenbach that things are off to an unusual start, that the world is strangely distorted, as if in a dream. As the boat pulls away from the shore, he feels as if he were swimming.

The sky is gray, the wind is damp, and it soon begins to rain.

Resting in his deck chair, Aschenbach falls asleep as he daydreams about the old man and the man who sold him his ticket.

At lunch, Aschenbach sees the clerks, including the old man, again. They have been drinking with the captain.

When the weather does not improve, Aschenbach resigns himself to reaching a different Venice by sea than he has by land on previous trips. He thinks of an unnamed poet who once came to this maritime city and silently recites some of that poet's verse. Moved by the feelings that this poet articulated, Aschenbach wonders if an emotional adventure could be in store for him, too.

The boat stops in the Venetian lagoon to await a medical inspection.

While they are waiting, the patriotic and drunken clerks cheer the *bersaglieri*, the Italian sharpshooters, who are drilling nearby. It is repulsive to see what condition the old man is in now. He can hardly keep his balance, he buttonholes and teases everyone who comes near him, and he licks the corners of his mouth in a disgustingly ambiguous way. Aschenbach regards him crossly and once again feels as if the world were becoming strangely and grotesquely distorted. The boat resumes its trip, heading for San Marco, Saint Mark's Square.

Aschenbach sees this amazing square where the boat will land, with its fantastic architecture that includes the Doges' Palace (a *doge* was the chief magistrate of Venice); the Bridge of Sighs, which leads from the palace to the adjoining prison; and part of Saint Mark's Church, a Byzantine basilica. It occurs to him that arriving in Venice by land, at the train station, is like entering a palace through a back door.

The boat stops, and Aschenbach asks for a gondola to take him ashore. Waiting for his luggage to be unloaded, he is pestered by the old man. The man drunkenly bids him farewell. As he is sending his compliments to Aschenbach's *Liebchen* (sweetheart), his upper dentures fall onto his lower lip. Aschenbach escapes him and goes down the gangplank.

The gondola and Aschenbach's ride in it seem especially ominous. Mann notes that coffins are the only other things so black, adding that gondolas make one think of nocturnal adventures and of funerals and death. He also writes that gondolas have the softest and most relaxing seats in the world. Aschenbach hears the gondoliers arguing, but he enjoys his sweet and unaccustomed languor, closes his eyes, and wishes his ride might last forever.

It grows increasingly quiet, and all that Aschenbach hears, besides the waves, is the oar and the muttering of the gondolier. When Aschenbach looks up, he is surprised to find that the gondolier is taking him out to sea, and it seems to him that he must not relax too much.

He repeats his wish to be taken ashore, to the steamer landing, but he receives no answer.

He repeats this wish again and turns around to look at the gondolier. The man's physical features are brutal. He is wearing blue and has a yellow sash and a straw hat. With his blond mustache and his short, turned-up nose, he does not seem Italian. He is small but energetic. He exposes his white teeth, and he wrinkles his reddish eyebrows.

Aschenbach and the gondolier now have a curt, tense conversation. Aschenbach says he wants to go to Saint Mark's, then take a vaporetto, a small steamboat, to the Lido. The gondolier replies that a vaporetto does not carry luggage. Aschenbach recalls that this is true, but he cannot tolerate the gondolier's bad manners. He orders him to turn back, but the gondolier does not respond and continues rowing.

Aschenbach wonders what to do and decides to acquiesce. He sees no way to get what he wants, and he would rather rest. His seat seems to cast a spell of indolence, and even the thought that he has fallen into the hands of a criminal cannot rouse him. He is more annoyed by the possibility that the gondolier is simply out for money.

Another conversation now ensues. Aschenbach ask how much the ride will cost, and the gondolier answers simply that Aschenbach will pay. Aschenbach refuses to pay anything unless the gondolier takes him where he wants to go. The gondolier replies that he is doing so and that he is doing so well.

Aschenbach silently agrees. Even if you want my money, he thinks, and send me to Hades by hitting me with your oar, you will have ferried me well.

A boat carrying musicians waylays the gondola, and the men and women in it sing until Aschenbach gives them money. They then fall silent and go away.

When Aschenbach arrives at the Lido, two municipal officials are pacing on the shore. Aschenbach gets out of the gondola and goes to get change to pay the gondolier. When he returns, his luggage is unloaded, but gondola and gondolier have vanished.

An old man at the landing explains that the gondolier has no concession, that is, no license, and that he has fled. The old man adds that Aschenbach has come for nothing, and Aschenbach walks to his hotel.

Aschenbach enters the hotel and is shown to his room by its manager. He then goes to the window and looks out at the beach and the sea.

Mann notes that a solitary person's observations and experiences are both more blurred and more penetrating than those of someone who is sociable. Solitude occasions what is original, beautiful, and poetic, he writes, but it also occasions what is perverse, disproportionate, absurd, and forbidden. Accordingly, Aschenbach is still disturbed by thoughts of the old man and the gondolier. He silently greets the sea, freshens up, and goes downstairs.

He has tea and takes a stroll on the boardwalk. Then he fastidiously dresses for dinner. Waiting in the lobby, he regards his fellow guests.

He hears foreign languages and sees an international clientele. Polish is being spoken nearby.

It comes from a governess, three girls who seem between fifteen and seventeen, and a longhaired boy of perhaps fourteen. Aschenbach is amazed by the boy's perfect beauty. The boy's face reminds him of ancient Greek sculptures, and he cannot recall ever meeting with anything like it either in nature or in the fine arts. In contrast to his strictly kempt and drably attired sisters, the boy looks soft and tender. His hair looks like that of the *Spinario*, an ancient statue of a boy removing a thorn from his foot. His sailor suit makes him look rich and pampered. He is seated, and his posture is one of unforced decorum. His face is white, like ivory, and stands out against his golden hair. Aschenbach wonders if he is sickly or just spoiled.

Most of the guests go into the dining room, but the young Poles remain seated. Aschenbach stays, too.

The governess gets up and bows as the children's mother arrives. The mother is discreetly dressed in gray and adorned with pearls. Her bearing is cool and measured.

The siblings kiss their mother's hand and follow her to the dining room. The boy turns around, and his eyes meet Aschenbach's.

Aschenbach is strangely moved by what he has just seen. He hesitates for a few minutes, then he goes into the dining room and is shown to a table far from that of the Polish family.

During dinner, Aschenbach muses about abstract, transcendent things, about how human beauty arises, and about the problem of form and art. He then finds his thoughts shallow and useless. That night, his sleep is enlivened by dreams.

The sky is still cloudy the next morning, and there is a land-breeze. Aschenbach believes he smells the putrid odor of the lagoon.

He is annoyed and thinks of leaving. Bad weather forced him to flee Venice once before. If the wind does not change, he thinks, he will not be able to stay.

At breakfast, the Polish girls and their governess are sitting two tables away from him. The boy is absent.

Aschenbach smiles and addresses the still absent boy as "kleiner Phäake" (little Phaeacian). In Homer's *Odyssey*, the Phaeacians are a pleasure-loving people who host Odysseus on their island when he is ship-wrecked. Aschenbach recites a line about them from book 8 of that epic.

Aschenbach is still at breakfast when the boy arrives.

As he enters, his gait is extraordinarily graceful. Aschenbach is astounded by his profile and shocked by his truly godlike beauty. His head is the head of Eros, the Greek god of love, and it has the yellow glow of marble from the Aegean island of Paros. That marble was used by ancient Greek sculptors.

Aschenbach approves of the boy's appearance and thinks to himself that he will stay in Venice as long as the boy does. He goes to the beach, is shown to his cabana, and makes himself comfortable in his chaise longue.

The scene at the beach entertains and pleases him. Some people are elegantly dressed; others are naked. A sand castle built by children flies the flags of many nations. There is a large, jovial, and relaxed Russian family.

Aschenbach gazes at the sea, which he loves for profound reasons: he is an artist who seeks the peace of the simple and the vast, and who is drawn to the undivided, the immense, the eternal, and to nothingness. The beautiful boy appears, and when he sees the Russian family, a look of contempt comes over his face.

To Aschenbach, the boy's strong dislike of his Russian "enemy" makes him seem human and worth serious interest. At the time when the events of *Death in Venice* occur, Poland was divided among and dominated by Russia, Prussia, and Austria.

Aschenbach hears other children call the boy's name, which sounds to him like "Adgio" or "Adgiu."

He tries to write some letters but thinks it a shame not to enjoy his situation, and he turns to see what "Adgio" is doing.

He sees the boy playing at the sand castle along with several other children. One of them, another Pole, seems to be the boy's best friend. This second Polish boy, who is addressed as "Jaschu," kisses "Adgio."

Silently quoting a passage from Xenophon's *Memorabilia*, an ancient Greek work about the life of Socrates, Aschenbach advises Jascha to flee the effects of that kiss. Then he eats some strawberries, and he decides that "Adgio" is the vocative form of the name "Tadzio." The vocative is a grammatical case that indicates a person being addressed.

Aschenbach sees Tadzio swimming, then coming out of the water. The sight of the boy makes him think of myths. It is like poetry about primeval times, the origin of form, and the birth of gods.

Aschenbach does not forget that Tadzio is now lying nearby. As someone who creates beauty, he feels protective, paternal, and inclined toward someone who has it.

Back in his room, Aschenbach observes his gray hair and tired face in the mirror. He thinks of his fame and his success. In the elevator after lunch, he encounters Tadzio at close range. The boy's smile is indescribably sweet, but his teeth do not look healthy. Aschenbach takes satisfaction in the thought that the boy probably will not grow old.

In the afternoon, Aschenbach takes a vaporetto to San Marco and walks through the streets of Venice. This walk completely changes his mood.

The air is thick and humid, and it makes him feel horrible. In a remote square, he sits down at the edge of a fountain and realizes that he must leave Venice.

Aschenbach decides to go to another resort, one not far from Trieste. He takes a gondola through the labyrinthine canals. The gondolier tries to make him stop and buy things. The charm of this bizarre ride is thus broken by the mercenary spirit of Venice.

Aschenbach informs his hotel that he must leave early the next day. Before going to bed, he packs his bags.

The next morning, the air seems fresher and he regrets his decision to leave. It is too late to change his mind.

At breakfast, a porter tells him it is time to go and that the automobile waiting to take him to a motorboat cannot wait any longer. Aschenbach impatiently tells the porter to let that car convey his luggage and that he will take the vaporetto. Time is truly short, and just as he gets up to leave, Tadzio comes through the door.

As he crosses Aschenbach's path, the boy looks at him. Aschenbach silently bids him farewell. Then he leaves the hotel and makes his way to the vaporetto. His journey to the train station is painful.

Aschenbach is torn between psychological inclination and physical inability: he wants to stay but is unable to do so. His earlier regret is now grief, pain, and suffering. Tears come to his eyes, and he cannot stand the thought that he will never see Venice again.

At the station, Aschenbach feels that he can neither go nor stay. It is very late. He does and does not want to catch his train. He buys a ticket, but an employee of the hotel says that his trunk has been sent to Como, a city on Lake Como in northern Italy. It thus has been sent in the wrong direction.

Aschenbach is inwardly joyous and cheerful. He says he does not want to travel without his luggage, and he asks if the hotel company's motorboat is ready to take him back to the hotel. It is, so just twenty minutes after arriving at the train station, he is on his way back to the Lido.

Along the way, Aschenbach looks angrily resigned, but he feels as excited as a runaway boy and considers himself extremely lucky. He tells himself that all will be well again, that an accident has been avoided and an error corrected.

An automobile awaits him and takes him to his hotel, where he is greeted by the manager.

He is given a different but almost identical room.

Aschenbach sits down in an armchair and looks out the window, glad to be back again. Around noon, he sees Tadzio returning from the beach, and he admits that it was because of the boy that departing was so difficult.

Aschenbach now looks into himself. He appears revived, interested, and happy. He raises his head and makes a slowly turning and lifting motion with his arms, which hang loosely from those of the chair, as if he were indicating an opening and expansion. It is a readily welcoming and receptive gesture.

CHAPTER 4

Mann's fourth chapter tells how Aschenbach grows increasingly infatuated with Tadzio and how he gradually acknowledges his strong feelings. It does so in terms that are often taken from Greek mythology. Those terms include names of gods, goddesses, and other mythological figures. They describe the sun, the sea, and Aschenbach's new way of life, feelings, thoughts, and words, not to mention Tadzio and his smile. It is not always clear if these mythological terms occur to Aschenbach only, or if Mann himself finds them appropriate, too. In any case, they almost always have erotic connotations, and they thereby suggest that the love story told in *Death in Venice* is poetic and antique.

The chapter begins with a florid description of Aschenbach's days and evenings now. Day after day, Helios, the ancient Greek sun god, drives his golden chariot across the sky. The murmuring of the nocturnal sea enchants the soul.

Aschenbach is far from thinking that the recovery of his luggage is a reason to leave Venice. He unpacks and decides to linger indefinitely.

The regular rhythm of his life there quickly casts its spell on him. He is no lover of leisure, and he has always been eager to return to his daily work. This place charms him, however, relaxes his will, and makes him happy. When he thinks of his summer home in the mountains, where he wrestles with that work, it seems to him that he has been transported to Elysium. In Greek mythology, Elysium was an otherworldly place where the blessed lived happily after death.

Aschenbach sees Tadzio almost constantly, and he encounters him everywhere. Mornings at the beach afford ample opportunity for studying and devoting himself to the boy. This regular good fortune and the daily recurrence of favorable circumstances fill him with contentment and joy.

He gets up and goes to the beach early in the morning. Then he has three or four hours to look at Tadzio.

He sees the boy playing in the sun and the sand. He cannot understand a single word that Tadzio says, in Polish, but the words sound pleasant to him, and foreignness elevates the boy's speech to music.

He soon knows every line and pose of the boy's beautiful body, and there is no end to his admiration and tender sensual pleasure. That body seems the expression of discipline and mental precision. Is the severe and pure will that produced this divine sculpture not at work in Aschenbach, the literary artist, too? Mann asks this question, perhaps from Aschenbach's point of view.

Aschenbach's eyes embrace the noble figure standing at the edge of the sea, and he thinks he envisions beauty itself, form as divine thought, pure intellectual perfection of which a human image and likeness is here to be worshiped. He welcomes his intoxication. His intellect is in labor, his mind is exited, and he remembers thoughts taught to him in his youth but never enlivened by his own experience. Those thoughts are about sensuality, the soul, and the role of human beauty in helping recollect and contemplate intellectual forms. They come from Plutarch's *Erotikos*, an ancient Greek work about love.

The enthused Aschenbach now imagines the scene of Plato's *Phaedrus*, a dialogue about love, beauty, and rhetoric. He envisions Plato's Socrates teaching Phaedrus about desire and virtue. In Aschenbach's mind, Socrates distinguishes base men, who cannot think of eternal beauty when they see its human image, from noble ones, who are truly reverent and ecstatic when they see a godlike face or a perfect body. Socrates adds that beauty can be a noble or sensitive man's means—but only a means—to intellect. He also observes that the lover is more divine than the beloved.

Aschenbach has a pulsating thought and an exact feeling: that nature shudders with bliss when intellect pays homage to beauty. He suddenly wishes to write, wishes to produce. The occasion is almost indifferent. The intellectual world has been asked to opine on some problem of culture and taste. Aschenbach knows the topic from his own experience and cannot resist the urge to write about it. He wishes to work in Tadzio's presence, to take the boy's figure as the model for his style, and to transport the boy's beauty into the realm of intellect, as Zeus once bore the beautiful shepherd Ganymede to Olympus. He has never felt the pleasure of the word as sweetly, never known as certainly that Eros is in the word, as when he writes his short treatise in this way. As Aschenbach leaves the beach, he feels exhausted, even shattered, as if his conscience were accusing him after an excess.

The next morning, Aschenbach sees Tadzio on the way to the beach. He thinks of exchanging a few words, and he hastens his step and catches up with him. Then he feels his heart pounding, feels out of breath, and fears that he is following the boy too closely and that Tadzio will notice him. He gives up this attempt at conversation.

Talking with Tadzio might have sobered Aschenbach, Mann notes, but the aging writer does not want sobriety. His intoxication is too dear to him. He is also not inclined to analyze his motives and to decide whether his plan was foiled by his conscience or by his dissoluteness and weakness. He worries that someone may have observed his defeat and find him ridiculous. Joking about his fear, he then quotes Plutarch's *Erotikos*. He is too haughty to fear an emotion.

The thought of going home now never occurs to him. His only concern is that the Polish family might leave. All the refreshment that he would otherwise expend working is now consumed in intoxication and sentiment.

Aschenbach sleeps poorly and wakes up at dawn. He then watches the sunrise. It is described in terms borrowed from Greek mythology. Mann refers to Eos, the goddess of dawn, for example, as well as to her brother Helios, the god of the sun. Four men Eos seduced are also mentioned: her husband Tithonos, Kleitos, Kephalos, and Orion. Aschenbach senses a return of former feelings, of delightful vexations that had died in his strict professional life. As he slowly forms a name with his lips, he falls asleep.

His day is elevated and mythically transformed. He perceives clouds and waves, for example, as animals found in ancient Greek fables. Such objects are described with a reference to Poseidon, the Greek god of the sea, and an allusion to Pan, a god of fertility. When he looks at Tadzio, he sees Hyacinth, a beautiful boy killed when a discus thrown by Apollo was blown off course by Zephyr, the god of the west wind. Both gods loved the boy. Aschenbach also sees the hyacinth flower said to have sprung from his blood.

Mann notes that nothing is stranger or more ticklish than a relationship between people who know each other only with their eyes and who never greet or speak to each other. Commenting on the restlessness, curiosity, hysteria, and tense respect that exist between such people, he adds that yearning is the product of insufficient knowledge.

This insight is borne out by his plot. Aschenbach is filled with joy when he learns that the attention he pays to Tadzio is not unrequited. Their eyes sometimes meet, and when that happens, both are profoundly serious. Aschenbach betrays no emotion, and Tadzio seems too well mannered to look at him for long.

One evening, things are different. The Polish siblings and their governess return to the hotel. Aschenbach has anxiously been waiting for them. Tadzio looks even paler than usual. He is unspeakably beautiful, and Aschenbach painfully feels that words can only praise sensual beauty, not render it.

Tadzio's appearance is sudden. Aschenbach has no time to make his face look calm and dignified, so his joy, surprise, and admiration are obvious as his gaze meets that of the boy. Tadzio smiles, smiles at him. It is the smile of Narcissus, the beautiful Greek youth who fell in love with his own image reflected in a pool and who died for love of himself.

Aschenbach is so shaken that he hastily goes to the park at the rear of the hotel. "You must not smile that way," he utters. "Listen, no one is allowed to smile like that at anyone." Beside himself, he throws himself onto a bench. Leaning back, with his arms hanging down, he is overwhelmed, he shudders, and he whispers, "I love you."

CHAPTER 5

Mann's final chapter introduces something new: a cholera epidemic. This disease first came to Venice in mid-May, at just about the time when Aschenbach left Munich. It therefore seems to parallel or reflect his development. Mann does not draw any simple links or lessons, however, raising as many questions as he seems to answer. What is the exact relationship between the epidemic and Aschenbach's state of mind, between the external and internal events that Mann narrates? What are we to make of the last scene? Does it confirm that Aschenbach has fallen in disgrace, or does it imply that he has risen to a higher realm? Does it allow both these possibilities? Just as *Death in Venice* is often abstract, then, it sometimes seems ambiguous.

The fifth chapter first tells that Aschenbach makes some unsettling observations about the outside world. There seem to be fewer guests staying at his hotel, and he no longer hears the German language spoken there. The hotel barber lets slip that there is some malady in Venice.

One afternoon, Aschenbach follows the Poles into town. In Saint Mark's Square, he notices a sweet aroma that is reminiscent of misery, wounds, and suspicious cleanliness. He recognizes this smell, then sees posters warning the population not to eat oysters or mussels and not to use water from the canals. This edict is clearly euphemistic.

A shopkeeper whom he asks about this fatal smell answers that the police have taken a precautionary measure, perhaps unnecessarily, and that the weather and wind, the scirocco, are unhealthy. On his way back to the Lido, Aschenbach notices the smell on the vaporetto.

In German newspapers at the hotel, he finds rumors, numbers, official denials, and doubts about their veracity. He thinks one should keep quiet and is pleased with events taking place in the filthy alleys of Venice. According to Mann, this is because passion, like crime, is not compatible with everyday order. It welcomes confusion and affliction, and it takes advantage of them. Aschenbach is thus anxious to keep the city's secret, which is fused with his own. His only fear is that Tadzio could depart. If that happened, he would not know how to go on living.

Aschenbach no longer leaves seeing Tadzio to chance. He now pursues the boy. Once, during a mass in Saint Mark's Church, he sees Tadzio turn to look at him.

He lies in wait and watches the Poles leave the church, then he furtively follows them on their walk through Venice. His heart and head are drunken, and he obeys the demon, Mann notes, who takes pleasure in trampling human reason and dignity.

When the Poles then take a gondola, so does Aschenbach. He has his gondolier follow them at a distance, fettered by passion to the wake of their black barque. Along the way, he sees rotting walls, arabesque windows, a beggar who pretends to be blind, and an antiques dealer who hopes to cheat him. He feels as if he sees the voluptuous art that thrived in

Venice, as if he hears the soporific music composed there. He also recalls that the city is sick and that it keeps its sickness secret for the sake of profit.

Aschenbach wants only to pursue and dream of Tadzio and to imagine speaking tender words to him. Not even the most outlandish things can make him blush or feel embarrassed. Once, he leaned his head against the door of the boy's room, completely intoxicated and unable to leave, despite the danger of being caught in such an insane position.

Nonetheless, he sometimes stops and dimly considers the path he is taking. He has always wanted his ancestors to approve of his life, and he thinks of them. Involved in an impermissible experience, amid such exotic emotional excesses, he thinks of their sternness and manliness, and he smiles melancholically. He also thinks that he, too, has been a soldier and that art is a kind of war. His life, too, can be called manly and valiant, then, and it seems to him that Eros is particularly appropriate and partial to such a life. Was this god of love not highly respected by the bravest nations? Many ancient heroes willingly bore his yoke. Mann asks this question and makes this observation in a way suggesting that they occur to Aschenbach himself.

Aschenbach also directs his attention to the unclean events within Venice, to the adventure of the outside world that coincides with that of his heart and holds out hope for his passion. Obsessed with learning more about the epidemic, he reads in German newspapers assertions and denials of its scope and severity. Certainty is not to be had.

Aschenbach derives bizarre satisfaction from asking loaded questions of people in the know and forcing them, who are sworn to secrecy, to lie. Once he asks the hotel manager why Venice is being disinfected. The manager replies that the police mean to prevent any possible ill effects of the warm weather.

That evening, a small group of street singers performs in the garden in front of Aschenbach's hotel. This group consists of two men and two women.

Its star and head is the guitarist and baritone, a talented mime and an energetic comedian. The audience rewards his pranks with encouraging laughter. The Russian family is especially delighted and incites him to outdo himself.

Aschenbach is sipping pomegranate juice and soda. He eagerly listens to the bad music because passion makes one less particular. His face is frozen into a painful smile. He is sitting laxly but is inwardly tense, for Tadzio is six steps away. The boy is leaning gracefully on a balustrade, politely watching the singers. He sometimes looks over his shoulder at Aschenbach, who forces himself not to look back. Aschenbach is afraid of being conspicuous and suspect. Repeatedly, he has noticed that the women protecting Tadzio have called the boy away from him and intend to keep them from coming near each other.

The guitarist is singing a popular tune. He has a gaunt build, an emaciated face, a shabby hat, and red hair. His posture is brazen. He does not seem Venetian, but rather Neapolitan, half pimp and half comedian, brutal, daring, dangerous, and entertaining. He makes his banal song sound ambiguous and improper by suggestively using his face, body, eyes, and tongue, the last in the corner of his mouth. His neck is haggard, and his Adam's apple looks conspicuously large and naked. He is pug-nosed, and he has two defiant and domineering furrows between his reddish eyebrows. What truly catches Aschenbach's attention is that he smells strongly of phenol, a disinfectant.

When he finishes singing, this man starts collecting money. His smile reveals his strong teeth. The guests observe him with curiosity and disgust. The smell accompanies him to Aschenbach. No one else seems to give it a thought.

Aschenbach asks the man why Venice is being disinfected. He answers that the scirocco is oppressive and unhealthy. Aschenbach then asks him if there is any disease in the city. The man denies that there is. After Aschenbach sends him away, he is taken aside by two employees of the hotel, who quietly cross-examine him. It appears that he swears to have been discreet. Then he steps forward for one last song.

Aschenbach cannot remember ever hearing this song, a hit in an unintelligible dialect. Its refrain consists of laughter without words or instrumental accompaniment. Performed by the lead singer, this laughter is ridicule. He seems barely able to contain it, and when the guests laugh with him, he laughs even harder and points at them is if there were nothing funnier than they themselves.

Aschenbach is sitting up straight, as if attempting to defend himself or flee. But the laughter, the medicinal smell, and Tadzio's proximity seem interwoven in a dream-spell that embraces his head and his senses. In the general commotion, he dares to look at Tadzio, and he notices that the boy, too, in returning his gaze, remains serious, as if following his example. Aschenbach is disarmed and overwhelmed by this obedience. It also seems to him that Tadzio's chest is cramped. He again thinks that the boy is sickly and unlikely to grow old. He is filled with both concern and satisfaction.

As the street singers leave, their leader performs further antics. Finally, he sticks out his tongue at the applauding guests. Those guests leave, too, and Tadzio no longer stands at the balustrade. Aschenbach remains seated at his table, though, with the rest of his pomegranate juice. The night progresses. Time disintegrates. There had been an hourglass in his parents' house, and he sees it in his imagination. The sand is running out of the top bulb and through the neck.

The next afternoon, Aschenbach takes a further step to tempt the outside world.

He enters an English travel bureau and, after changing some money, asks a clerk there about the epidemic. The young Briton starts to give him the same answer he has heard before. When he sees Aschenbach's expression of disgust, though, he blushes. Then he tells him the truth.

The clerk reveals the course of the epidemic, the number of cases, the symptoms of cholera, the Venetian authorities' duplicity and corruption, and an increase in crime and prostitution. Asiatic cholera, he explains, has been spreading for several years. It started in the delta of the Ganges River, a primeval wilderness where tigers crouch in bamboo thickets. It then spread to the rest of India, to China, to Afghanistan and Persia, to Russia, to Mediterranean France and Spain, and to Sicily and southern Italy. The first two cases of it in Venice occurred in the middle of May and were soon followed by ten, twenty, and thirty more. An Austrian tourist in Venice for pleasure died after returning home, showing its symptoms. The Venetian authorities claimed that sanitary conditions in the city had never been better, and they took measures necessary to fight the disease. The food supply was probably infected, though, and the early summer heat helped the disease spread. Instances of recovery were rare, and most people died in a horrible way, since the disease frequently appeared in its most dangerous form, the one called "dry." The city hospital and the orphanages were full, and traffic to the island of San Michele, the cemetery, was heavy. But fear of losing the tourists' business proved stronger than the love of truth and respect for international agreements, and the authorities kept up their policy of silence and denial. The highest medical bureaucrat indignantly resigned and was replaced by someone more pliant. The people of Venice knew about this, and the corruption of their officials, together with their uncertainty and state of emergency, demoralized the lower classes and encouraged antisocial drives. Public drunkenness, robberies and murders, and extreme forms of prostitution were seen.

The English clerk advises Aschenbach to leave Venice sooner rather than later. In a few days, he explains, the city is sure to be quarantined.

In possession of the truth, Aschenbach paces up and down Saint Mark's Square. He considers doing something purifying and decent: warning Tadzio's mother that Venice is infected and telling her to depart with Tadzio and his sisters. But he feels infinitely far from earnestly wanting to take such a step, for it would bring him back to his senses. He thinks of the mortuary chapel and the wanderer, and the thought of returning home—of reflection, sobriety, effort, and mastery—is so repulsive that his face becomes distorted in an expression of physical illness. "One should keep quiet," he says. "I shall keep quiet." The consciousness of his complicity intoxicates him, and his image of the plagued city ignites hopes beyond reason, hopes that are monstrously sweet. He remains silent and stays.

That night, he has a terrible dream. The scene of its events is his soul, and those events crush his resistance, devastating and destroying his life and cultivation.

The dream starts with fear, desire, and horrified curiosity. Aschenbach's senses harken, for a tumult, din, and mixture of noise is nearing from afar: rattling, crashing, thundering, cries of joy, the howling of a drawn-out *u*-sound, and flute playing that charms the entrails. He knows what is coming: "The foreign god!" He then recognizes mountainous terrain like that surrounding his summerhouse, and a swarm, a raging mob, of people and animals floods the slope with bodies, flames, tumult, and dancing. Women shake tambourines, swing torches, and hold snakes as well as their breasts in their hands. Men wearing horns and furs play cymbals and hit drums. Boys prod goats. All howl a cry that has the drawn-out *u* at the end. Aschenbach's disgust is great, as is his fear, and as is his will to protect himself against the foreign enemy of composed and dignified intellect. But the noise swells to madness. The odor of goats, of bodies, of putrefying water, and of wounds and illness assaults his senses. His heart pounds; his head spins; he is seized with rage, blindness, and lust; and his soul longs to join in the dance. The celebrants reveal and raise their obscene symbol, a huge wooden thyrsus that stands for Dionysus. Foaming at the mouth, they stimulate each other, stab each other's flesh, and lick each other's blood. Aschenbach is now with them, in them, and enthralled to the foreign god. They are Aschenbach himself as they throw themselves onto the animals and devour steaming gobs of flesh, as a limitless mingling begins on the trampled ground. And his soul tastes the indecency and the rave of going under.

When Aschenbach awakens, he is enervated, shattered, and powerless. He no longer cares if people see or suspect him. And they are fleeing, departing anyway. It seems that the truth has seeped out and that panic can no longer be delayed. But the Polish family stays, Tadzio stays, and it sometimes seems to Aschenbach that fleeing and death could remove all life around him and that he could remain alone with the beautiful boy. When he stares at Tadzio and follows him, the monstrous seems promising, and moral law invalid.

Like any lover, Aschenbach wishes to please. He adds youthful accessories to his clothing, puts on jewels, and uses perfume. In view of the youth that delights him, he is disgusted by his aging body. He is driven to refresh and restore himself. He frequently visits the hotel barber.

On one of these visits, it is torture for him to observe his gray hair in the mirror. The unctuous barber flatters him, tells him that one is as old as one feels, and offers to dye his hair. He does so, and Aschenbach's hair turns black again.

The barber then freshens up the skin on Aschenbach's face. He applies makeup to Aschenbach's eyes, rouge to his skin, and color to his lips. His furrows and wrinkles disappear. Looking at himself in the mirror, Aschenbach sees the bloom of youth. The barber tells him that he can now fall in love. As he leaves, Aschenbach is enchanted. His tie is red, and there is a multi-colored band around his straw hat.

The air is humid, thick, and full of putrid smells. To the fevering Aschenbach, it seems that Harpies are about, mythical monsters shaped like birds, wind-spirits that eat and defile the food of the condemned. This is because the sultriness checks his appetite, and because it occurs to him that food in Venice is poisoned with infectious substances.

One afternoon, on the trail of the beautiful boy, Aschenbach is deep in the tangle of the sick city. His sense of direction is failing, and he is unaware of the fatigue and the exhaustion that emotion and constant tension have caused his body and his mind. He is determined not to lose sight of Tadzio, who occasionally turns to assure himself that his lover is following. He sees Aschenbach, and he does not betray him. Aschenbach steals after his unseemly hope but is cheated out of it. After the Poles cross an arched bridge, he cannot find them. Enervation and frailty finally force him to abandon his search.

Burning, sweaty, trembling, and thirsty, he looks around for refreshment. He buys and eats some soft, overripe strawberries. He recognizes a small square. It was here, weeks ago, that he vainly planned to flee. He sinks down onto the steps of the cistern in the middle of the square and rests his head on its rim. Trash is lying about. Behind the windows of one of the houses he sees emptiness, and a pharmacy is on the ground floor of another. Gusts of wind smell like phenol.

He sits there, the master, the artist, the author, the high-achiever, he whose fame is official, whose name is ennobled, and from whose style schoolboys are encouraged to learn. He sits there with his eyes closed, and his slack lips form individual words out of the strange dream-logic produced by his half-slumbering brain.

Aschenbach again imagines snippets of Plato's *Phaedrus,* which he conflates with his own idea that artists, whose path to things intellectual leads through the senses, can never achieve true wisdom and dignity. This path, according to his dream, is sweet but dangerous, a path of error and sin, and one that necessarily leads all who take it astray. We poets cannot take the path of beauty, he thinks, without being accosted by Eros. In our way, we may be heroes and warriors, but we are like women, for we are elated by passion and we yearn for love. We must remain dissolute and adventurers of emotion. The masterly attitude of our style is a lie and folly, our fame and honor are a farce, and the masses' trust in us is supremely ridiculous. Educating the people and the young by means of art is a risky undertaking that should be forbidden. Artists naturally incline to the abyss. We renounce knowledge, for knowledge has no dignity and discipline. It has sympathy for the abyss. It *is* the abyss. So we reject it and strive for beauty, that is to say, for simplicity, grandeur, and new discipline, for reborn naiveté, and for form. But form and naiveté lead to intoxication and to desire. They, too, lead to the abyss. We poets are not capable of pulling ourselves together, only of falling apart.

A few days later, Aschenbach feels ill. He is struggling with dizzy spells that are accompanied by fear and bewilderment, by a feeling of inescapability and hopelessness. He cannot tell if this feeling has to do with the external world or with his own existence. In the lobby of the hotel, he finds out that the Polish family will leave that afternoon. He goes to the sea.

It is inhospitable there. It seems autumnal and outmoded. This place of pleasure is almost empty. A camera on a tripod stands abandoned at the edge of the sea. A black cloth hanging over it flutters in the wind.

Resting in his chaise longue, Aschenbach watches Tadzio and his friends at play. The Polish women are not there to supervise them, and their games degenerate. Jascha forces Tadzio into a wrestling match, which quickly ends in the defeat of the beautiful, weaker boy. Jascha then presses Tadzio's face into the sand for so long that Tadzio is in danger of suffocating. Tadzio's attempts to shake him off are spasmodic. Jascha finally releases his victim. Tadzio sits motionless for several minutes, then gets up and slowly goes away. He rejects Jascha's attempt to make amends, and walks down to the water.

He lingers at the edge of the sea, then wades to a sandbar. He stands there for a moment, facing the distance, then strides along the narrow stretch of ground. Separated from the land by the water, and from his playmates by his pride, he wanders in the sea and in the wind, in front of the nebulous limitlessness. Again, he stops to look outward. Suddenly, as if remembering something, or on an impulse, he turns his upper body and looks at the beach. Aschenbach is sitting there, just as he was when Tadzio first looked back at him from the threshold of the dining room. Aschenbach's head has slowly been turning to follow Tadzio's movements. It rises now, as if meeting the boy's gaze, then falls onto his chest, while his countenance shows the expression of a deep slumber. It seems to him as if the pale and lovely psychagogue, a conductor of human souls, were smiling at him, waving at him, as if he were pointing out and hovering ahead of him into the promising and the enormous. As so often, Aschenbach sets out to follow him.

Minutes pass until Aschenbach, collapsed in his chair, is helped. He is carried to his room. That same day, a respectfully shaken world receives the news of his death.

3   Texts

Death in Venice consists of words that originated in specific circumstances and that have been published in differing forms. How those words originated—their genesis, that is—has to do with their author's own trip to the Adriatic in the spring of 1911 and with his writing them over the course of the following year. One can understand this genesis, at least in part, by reading the essays and some of the letters Mann composed then and by studying the notes he made in preparation for his story. The forms in which his words have been published—their editions, that is—include two German and eight English versions. One can appreciate how such editions vary by comparing the wording of one particular passage in the German originals as well as in the English translations. It helps to know both these things, both how Mann's words came into being and how they have appeared in print, when one tries to decide what his novella means. The complexity of his hero becomes apparent, for example, as does the subtleness of his literary language.

GENESIS

Mann in Venice

Death in Venice was outwardly occasioned during a trip to Venice that Mann took in May 1911. He went there with his wife, Katia, and his brother, Heinrich. The three first vacationed on Brioni, an island off the coast of Istria, a peninsula in the Adriatic. At that time, Istria, which is now in Croatia, still belonged to Austria. The Manns left Brioni on 26 May and took a boat from Pola, a seaport near the southern tip of Istria, to Venice. They stayed at the Hôtel des Bains on the Lido, returning to Mann's summer home in the Bavarian spa town of Bad Tölz on 2 June.

Many of the fictional events recounted in Mann's story resemble the actual ones that took place on his trip. In an autobiographical sketch published in 1930, he recalled that nothing in that story is invented. The wanderer at the cemetery, the ship from Pola, the old dandy, the dubious gondolier, Tadzio and his family, an attempt to depart that was stymied by lost luggage, the honest clerk, and the street singer—all had existed in fact. Nonetheless, it is hardly true, of course, that nothing in *Death in Venice* is made up. Among other things, the luggage lost on the Manns' vacation belonged to Heinrich, not Thomas. Unlike Aschenbach, more-over, Thomas survived Venice and went back home. He did, however, see a beautiful Polish boy there. This boy was the young Władysław Moes, a baron who, beginning in the mid-1960s, confirmed that he had been the model for Tadzio. Mann's trip to Venice thus furnished many characters and details found in his story, above all the sight of a beautiful youth that lies at its core.

One of the events that transpired during that trip was the death of the Austrian composer Gustav Mahler (1860–1911). Mahler, whom Mann had met in Munich in 1910, died in Vienna on 18 May 1911. At that time, Mann was on Brioni. He later recalled that he followed daily news-paper reports about the composer's condition. A photograph of Mahler that he cut from a newspaper, in fact, is the source of his detailed descrip-tion of Aschenbach's physical features at the end of chapter 2. Aschen-bach bears Mahler's first name, too. Finally, Mahler died when he was fifty, and Aschenbach, even though Mann never gives his exact age in *Death in Venice,* was ennobled when he turned fifty. In these superficial ways, Mahler thus served as a historical model for Aschenbach.

A further and a far more significant real-life model for Mann's protago-nist was another, German composer: Richard Wagner (1813–83). Wagner wrote part of his opera *Tristan und Isolde* (1865) in Venice. Mann seems to allude to this fact in chapter 5 when he has Aschenbach recall seduc-tive and soporific music composed there. The final aria of *Tristan und Isolde,* in fact, may hold a clue to how Aschenbach perishes. That famous aria is sung by Isolde over the dead body of Tristan, her extramarital lover in medieval Cornwall. It seems to Isolde that Tristan is smiling, just as in Mann's last scene it seems to Aschenbach as if Tadzio is smiling at him. Isolde also wonders if the melody that she hears coming from Tristan consists of waves of air and billows of fragrance. In Mann's scene, Tadzio stands in front of the sea at a beach where the wind blows and the water curls. What is more, Isolde perceives that Tristan is rising to a higher realm. Mann says nothing comparable, but the similarities between his ultimate scene and Wagner's—the beloved's apparent smile and the indications, near the sea, of wind and waves—would seem to invite the interpretation that Aschenbach's death is likewise elevating. In any case, Isolde now wills her own death. Indeed, her aria is known as her *Liebestod* (love-death). Aschenbach appears to die in a similar way, in illicit and powerful love. What is more, Wagner died in Venice, as does Aschenbach. With his death no less than with his opera, then, he seems to have furnished another model for Mann's story.

Wagner and his music are important to *Death in Venice* in further ways as well. On stationery from the very hotel where he lodges Aschenbach, Mann wrote an essay eventually entitled *Über die Kunst Richard Wagners* (On the Art of Richard Wagner, 1911). In this essay, Mann distances himself from Wagner, expressing mixed feelings about his music. As an artist, Wagner once seemed irresistible, Mann recalls, although the nobility, purity, and healthiness of his "effects" seemed deeply questionable. His star is now sinking, Mann adds, even though his popularity is at a high point among the bourgeois public. In *Death in Venice*, Mann says similar things about Aschenbach. He, too, is an artist respected by bourgeois audiences, an artist whose nobility seems suspect, however, and whose fame is waning, at least in his own mind. What is more, Mann calls Wagner the "representative" artist of the nineteenth century. A twentieth-century masterpiece would differ from his operas, Mann adds, for such a masterpiece would be logical, formal, and clear, a work that is at once strict and serene, cooler and healthier. The beauty of this masterpiece would not lie in intoxication. In short, Mann calls for a new classicality. It appears that Aschenbach, and even Mann himself, may have aspired to this neoclassicism. There are certainly many allusions or references in *Death in Venice* to the life, art, and myths of ancient Greece. It is not always clear whether Mann himself is making them—making them directly, that is—or merely having Aschenbach do so. In many instances, though, they expose Aschenbach's aestheticism, his belief in beauty, to be shallow and misleading. What is more, ancient Greece turns out to be the home of forces for, and not just against, intoxication. Espousing a new classicality thus proves to be more complicated in Mann's story than it seems in his essay on Wagner. In any case, he wrote that essay in response to a kind of questionnaire, just as Aschenbach writes his treatise. He also wrote it, as noted above, on stationery from his hotel, which was the same one at which Aschenbach stays, the Hôtel des Bains. This parallel hardly proves that Aschenbach is Mann, of course, or that Aschenbach's treatise, too, concerns Wagner. Mann never says precisely what the subject of that treatise is. He merely states that Aschenbach has been asked to give his opinion on some current problem of culture and taste. That Mann wrote about Wagner, however, and called for a new classicality in circumstances so similar to those of his hero, suggests the importance of this composer and of this artistic agenda in his story. Not only Aschenbach's death, then, but also his dubious stature and classical inclinations seem to have been related, in Mann's way of thinking, to Wagner.

Mann's essay on Wagner is important to *Death in Venice* in another way, too. In it, Mann confesses admiration for Wagner's narrative means, especially the recurrent themes known as "leitmotifs." Such motifs abound in *Death in Venice*, most notably in the series of sinister male characters, who often have similar features. The wanderer at the cemetery in Munich, the gondolier who ferries Aschenbach to the Lido, and the street singer at Aschenbach's hotel, for example, all are lean, and each has a pug nose, red or reddish eyelashes or eyebrows, and prominent teeth. All wear similar hats, too, and none seems native to his surroundings. For that matter, both the wanderer and the gondolier have yellow items of clothing, while the wanderer and the singer alike have furrows between their brows, wear sport shirts, and possess Adam's apples described as naked. These three men do not look identical, but they look strikingly similar. They thus seem to be variations on a single pattern, and they link the beginning, middle, and end of Mann's story. To the extent that Mann derived this technique from Wagner, who used such recurring motifs in his music, Wagner's operas are models for Mann's storytelling. Mann himself says as much in his essay, though he also observes that, in other artistic respects, Wagner had nothing to teach him. Mann's attitude toward Wagner is ambivalent, then, but the narrative structure of *Death in Venice* owes a great deal to his lasting appreciation of Wagner's music dramas. This is yet another conclusion that can be drawn from the essay on Wagner that Mann wrote during his trip to Venice.

Mann's Letters

Letters that Mann wrote after returning home from this trip give us a good idea of what was on his mind during the year or so that it took him to compose his novella. Writing to Hans von Hülsen from Bad Tölz on

3 July 1911, one month after he got back from Venice, Mann noted that he had finished an essay on the French-German author and poet Adelbert von Chamisso (1781–1838) and had decided to start "a difficult, if not impossible novella."[1] In that essay, Mann comments that the moral of the romantic Chamisso's most famous tale, *Peter Schlemihls wundersame Geschichte* (Peter Schlemihl's Wondrous Story, 1814) is "Songez au solide!", that is, think well of bourgeois solidity and belonging to human society. Mann also observes that Chamisso, after writing this tale, settled down and was revered as a master. This comment and this observation seem to foreshadow what Aschenbach has done before Mann's readers meet him. He, too, is an author who has taken his place in a bourgeois world that honors his artistic mastery. Is it "difficult, if not impossible" for him, however, to play such a respectable social role?

Mann seems to have had another, closely related problem in mind when on 18 July 1911, two weeks later, he wrote to Philipp Witkop, again from Bad Tölz. He reports that he is now working on *Death in Venice*, and he anticipates Witkop's disapproval of its subject of sexual love between a man and a boy: "I am in the midst of a work: a really strange thing that I brought with me from Venice, a novella, serious and pure in tone, concerning a case of pederasty in an aging artist. You say, 'Hum, hum!' but it is quite respectable."[2] Despite its chaste and sober manner of expression, the erotic content of his story thus seems to have been a further reason why Mann had difficulty writing it. In any case, he is concerned with respectability here, too.

Whatever his reason for thinking that his novella was so difficult, Mann called it impossible in two other letters as well. In the first, dated 16 October 1911 and addressed to Ernst Bertram from Munich, he said, "I am tormented by a work, which, in the process of its execution, has evermore proved itself to be an impossible conception."[3] Mann also remarks that he has already spent too much effort on this work to give it up. By then, in mid-October, he had been writing it for over three months. By the end of that month, he thought that he was making good progress, but in the second letter, dated 11 December 1911 and addressed to Wilhelm Herzog, he explained again that *Death in Venice* seemed impossible and that writing it tormented him. As he put it, "I am occupied to the point of torment with a novella that is perhaps an impossible conception."[4]

In the early months of 1912, Mann's attitude toward his project began to change. Instead of telling his correspondents how difficult the novella was, he started to suggest that he was satisfied with it. Writing to von

Hülsen again, on 7 February 1912, he hinted that it would turn out to be something significant. To his brother Heinrich, he expressed similar, understated hopes for its success. Writing to him from Munich on 2 April 1912, he said: "It's at least something very strange, and if you're unable to approve of it in its entirety, at least you won't be able to deny some instances of its beauty. A classicizing chapter seems especially to be a success."[5] From Thomas's remark that Heinrich might disapprove of the novella as a whole and acknowledge its beauty only grudgingly, one senses the sibling rivalry between these fellow authors, whose ideas about the function of art and the role of literature often differed dramatically. The "classicizing chapter" is chapter 4, which enriches Aschenbach's story with many allusions to Greek mythology. In this same letter, Thomas also told Heinrich that he hoped to finish the novella by the beginning of May. In fact, he did not do so until July. The genesis of *Death in Venice* thus lasted a year and two months, from May 1911 to July 1912.

In the course of his long life, Mann wrote many other letters that discuss *Death in Venice*. Many of them include his own, sometimes conflicting, interpretations of it. One is from 14 October 1912, from the month in which his novella was first published. This letter, written from Bad Tölz, is addressed to Hedwig Fischer, the wife of his publisher, Samuel Fischer. In it, Mann hopes she will not be disappointed by the second half of his story. He explains what, tragically, happens to Aschenbach: "It does not have a positive ending; the dignity of the 'hero and poet' is completely destroyed. It is a real tragedy."[6] As in his essay on Chamisso, which he wrote just before starting *Death in Venice*, Mann, in this letter written not long after he finished it, mentions the dignity of a literary artist.

This is an issue that Mann also often raised with regard to another author whom he had in mind while writing *Death in Venice*: Johann Wolfgang von Goethe (1749–1832). In several letters that he wrote over the course of many years, Mann claims that he had originally intended to tell how the elderly Goethe lost his dignity by falling in love with the young Ulrike von Levetzow (1804–99) at Marienbad, the Bohemian spa, in the early 1820s. He made this same claim in *On Myself*, a lecture he gave to students at Princeton University in May 1940. As he explains in that lecture, he wished to show how an accomplished intellect was degraded by a passion for a piece of charming, innocent life. For Goethe, he added, this episode caused a severe emotional crisis, a death before he died. Mann's novella turned out differently. It is not about Goethe, and it tells of homoerotic, not heterosexual, love. Nonetheless, his initial plan persisted insofar as *Death in Venice* describes an encounter between intellect and life. If one sees the novella in such abstract terms, it appears to be far more than just a fateful love story. In any case, Aschenbach seems to possess traits of several musical or literary men: Mann himself, Mahler, Wagner, Chamisso, and Goethe.

Mann's Working Notes

Like Mann's letters, his working notes for *Death in Venice* reveal much about the genesis of his story. Those notes include his own preliminary ideas and words, a letter from an acquaintance in Paris, articles clipped from newspapers, and a photograph of Mahler. They also include Mann's excerpts and paraphrases of German translations of Homer's *Odyssey*, Plato's *Phaedrus* and *Symposium*, Virgil's *Aeneid*, and Plutarch's *Erotikos*. Furthermore, they contain passages from Friedrich Nösselt's *Lehrbuch der griechischen und römischen Mythologie* (1828), a book on Greek and Roman mythology; from Erwin Rohde's *Psyche* (1890–94), a book about ancient Greek beliefs in the soul and immortality; from Georg Lukács's *Die Seele und die Formen* (The Soul and the Forms, 1911), a collection of essays; and from the poetry and prose of Friedrich Schiller (1759–1805). In these notes, Mann describes his main characters, both Aschenbach and Tadzio; records facts about Greek mythology and the Greeks' ideas of beauty, pederasty, and divinely inspired madness; and gathers information on Asiatic cholera. A knowledge of those notes can therefore help readers understand his novella.

Mann's remarks on his principal characters are brief but helpful. His calculations suggest that Aschenbach is fifty-three years old, that the events of *Death in Venice* occur in 1911, and that Aschenbach was therefore born in 1858. In the novella, his birthplace is said to be "L"; one of Mann's notes hints that this letter stands for Liegnitz, a city in Silesia, which is a province now mostly in Poland. Another note cites Aschenbach's motto, "Trotzdem" (Despite), and describes him as a heroic Hamlet. This same note tells how his prose style developed, becoming firm, traditional, academic, and conservative. Mann also outlines links between chapter 2 and chapter 5, between Aschenbach's rise to dignity and his erotic passion. Form is sin, Mann writes, and the surface is the abyss. Death alone saves Aschenbach's dignity, he observes, and the fact that Aschenbach was ennobled is ironic. Mann sketches his hero's itinerary, too, having him depart Munich on 22 May, then spend ten days on Brioni, and be in the fourth week of his vacation in Venice around

27 June. It is striking that Mann, in his story itself, used almost all of his initial ideas about Aschenbach's career, but that he eliminated most of his references to specific times and places.

Mann seldom mentions Tadzio in his notes. Describing the boy's smile as that of Narcissus, as he does in the novella as well, he does say that Tadzio sees his reflection in Aschenbach's face, sees the effects of his own beauty. One note, moreover, reveals a bit about Tadzio's name. That note consists of a letter written to Mann by a painter in Paris named Olga Meerson. Mann had apparently asked her to help him determine the name of the Polish boy he admired on the Lido. Meerson writes that "Adgiu," the name Mann thought he heard, is actually "Tadzio," which is short for "Tadeusz." She thinks that he may have heard "Władzio," which is short for "Władysław," but says "Tadzio" is much prettier. Actually, as noted above, the boy on the beach was indeed named "Władysław."

The bulk of Mann's working notes for *Death in Venice* concerns Greek mythology and Greek notions of love, beauty, and enthusiasm. Many of those notes simply define mythological creatures, figures, or places: Harpies, the Elysian Fields, Eos, Ganymede, Hyacinth, Apollo, Poseidon, Dionysus, Amor, and Mercury. Dionysus seems especially important. According to Mann's notes, he is not simply a god of wine and intoxication, but also a foreign, Asiatic fertility god. He is accompanied by a wild retinue and strikes with madness and fatal illnesses people who do not pay him homage. Mann's notes also include long excerpts from Plutarch's *Erotikos* and from Plato's *Phaedrus* and *Symposium*. These Greek works are about the nature and the effects of love. The excerpts from Plutarch treat the enthusiasm, the divinely inspired madness, of love, especially of pederasty, the love of men for boys. This love is said to inspire bravery in soldiers. Those excerpts also say that the sun turns our thoughts from intellectual to sensual things and that the soul can learn the true nature of things only in the intellectual world, the site of true beauty. Amor leads the soul to intellectual objects, which it can approach only with the help of a body. In other words, love uses beautiful youths to make the divine and the intellectual visible and to remind us of such elevated objects. To virtuous, decent people, sensual beauty thus serves as a reminder of a higher, intellectual kind. The excerpts from Plato raise similar issues. In them, Mann quotes passages about the power of Eros and about how noble homosexual love leads those who feel it to intellectual beauty, to virtue, and to wisdom. Many of these passages recur, sometimes verbatim, in *Death in Venice* itself. Furthermore, Mann notes how the ancient Greeks conceived of ecstasy and enthusiasm. He excerpts Rohde's remark that, for them, madness was a corollary of measure and of form. This statement suggests how closely the extremes of Aschenbach's behavior—his sensual surrender and his artistic control—are related.

Finally, Mann's notes for *Death in Venice* include detailed information on Asiatic cholera. They cite its pathology, symptoms, and treatment; mortality rates and results of autopsies; and the hygienic measures taken to counter its spread, including quarantines. Mann records information about its origin in the delta of the Ganges River in India, and about several nineteenth-century epidemics in Europe. He seems to take special interest in outbreaks that occurred in the northern German city of Hamburg and in Venice. His notes include a newspaper article about the epidemic that struck Palermo, Sicily, in the summer of 1911.

Mann's working notes thus show his story emerging both from his own thoughts and from his several primary as well as secondary sources. Before writing it, he not only recorded those thoughts, but also did his homework. In his notes, one therefore finds a wealth of philosophical, historical, and medical information, not to mention all his miscellaneous jottings. Accordingly, one sees some of the many things beyond his own experience that found their way into *Death in Venice*. There, of course, Mann transforms such raw material into a highly artful literary fiction.

EDITIONS

German Editions

The first German editions of *Death in Venice* were related in complex ways. The novella was initially published in *Die Neue Rundschau*, a German literary magazine. It appeared in the issues for October and November of 1912. The text printed there is the same one that was published as a book by Samuel Fischer in Berlin in 1913. This text is also the one that has been reprinted in almost all subsequent editions. In Munich, Hans von Weber meanwhile published a limited luxury edition that is dated 1912. The text of this luxury edition is considered inferior to that of Fischer's because Mann revised some passages that von Weber had already printed.[7] The most important differences between the two occur in the passage describing the vision Aschenbach has while waiting for the streetcar at the cemetery in Munich. In the later version, Mann suggests how powerful and immediate that vision is, largely by relating it in a single sentence and by removing traces of his own narrative voice. The earlier version includes a few words reminding its readers of that voice, and it consists of three sentences rather than just one. The first German editions of *Death in Venice* thus differ slightly but significantly.

In German, *Death in Venice* has appeared in other editions as well, most notably in collections of Mann's works, collections published by Fischer in Frankfurt am Main. It is in volume 8 of his *Gesammelte Werke in dreizehn Bänden* (1974), for example, and in the volume *Frühe Erzählungen* in his *Gesammelte Werke in Einzelbänden* (1981). The most thoroughly annotated edition of the novella was prepared by T. J. Reed and published by Hanser in Munich in 1983. This edition contains not only the text of *Death in Venice*, but also Mann's previously unpublished working notes and Reed's commentary on its interpretation, reception, and place in Mann's oeuvre, as well as Reed's own notes, his further remarks, and a bibliography. An annotated edition of Mann's works, letters, and diaries has recently begun to be published by Fischer in eighty-five volumes. It will, of course, include *Death in Venice*. There are also several illustrated German editions.

The German text of *Death in Venice* has also been published in editions designed for English-speaking students. These editions usually include an introduction and notes in English, a glossary, and a bibliography. Such helpful editions have been prepared by A. W. Hornsey (1969), T. J. Reed (1971), and George E. Boyd and Henry M. Rosenwald (1973).[8]

English Translations

To date, eight translations of *Death in Venice* exist in English. They are the work of Kenneth Burke (whose first translation was later revised), H. T. Lowe-Porter, David Luke, Clayton Koelb, Stanley Appelbaum, Joachim Neugroschel, and Jefferson S. Chase. It is illuminating to compare these seven translators' results. Consider, for example, their different versions of the same passage mentioned above in the comparison of the first two German editions, the passage about the tropical landscape that Aschenbach envisions just after he sees the wanderer at the cemetery in Munich. The translations are presented here in chronological order, according to their dates of publication. Not all of their variations can be analyzed here, of course, and this passage is only a small part of Mann's text. Nonetheless, comparing them gives one a good idea of how the translations differ on the whole. Doing so also gives one a far better sense of what Mann wrote in German. Needless to say, much is necessarily lost in any translation of fiction as subtle and complex as *Death in Venice*.

Consider first the translation done by Kenneth Burke. That translation initially appeared in *The Dial*, an American literary magazine, in 1924. It was published as a book in 1925, then revised in 1970. Differences between its earlier and later versions show both why one needs to render

Mann's meaning accurately and how difficult that can be. Here is the original version of 1924 and 1925:

> His yearnings crystallized; his imagination, still in ferment from his hours of work, actually pictured all the marvels and terrors of a manifold world which it was suddenly struggling to conceive. He saw a landscape, a tropical swampland under a heavy, murky sky, damp, luxuriant and enormous, a kind of prehistoric wilderness of islands, bogs, and arms of water, sluggish with mud; he saw, near him and in the distance, the hairy shafts of palms rising out of a rank lecherous thicket, out of places where the plant-life was fat, swollen, and blossoming exorbitantly; he saw strangely misshapen trees lowering their roots into the ground, into stagnant pools with greenish reflections; and here, between floating flowers which were milk-white and large as dishes, birds of a strange nature, high-shouldered, with crooked bills, were standing in the muck, and looking motionlessly to one side; between dense, knotted stalks of bamboo he saw the glint from the eyes of a crouching tiger—and he felt his heart knocking with fear and with puzzling desires.[9]

And here is the revision of 1970:

> His yearnings took visual form; his imagination, still in ferment from his hours of work, actually pictured all the marvels and terrors of a manifold world which it was suddenly struggling to conceive. He saw a landscape, a tropical swampland under a heavy, murky sky, damp, luxuriant and enormous, a kind of primeval wilderness of islands, bogs, and arms of water, sluggish with mud; he saw, near him and in the distance, the hairy shafts of palms rising out of a rank voluptuous thicket, out of places where the plant life was fat, swollen, and blossoming exorbitantly; he saw strangely misshapen trees lowering their roots into the ground, into stagnant pools with greenish reflections; and here, between floating flowers which were milk-white and large as dishes, birds of a strange nature, high-shouldered, with crooked bills, were standing in the muck, and looking motionlessly to one side; between dense, knotted stalks of bamboo he saw the glint from the eyes of a crouching tiger—and he felt his heart knock with fear and with puzzled desires.[10]

There are four differences between these original and revised versions of Burke's text. First, in the original version Aschenbach's yearnings "crystallized," but in the revision they "took visual form." This latter expression is more accurate. In his German, Mann says nothing about crystallizing. Furthermore, his phrase "Seine Begierde ward sehend" (His desire became seeing) indicates that the entire passage following this introductory phrase will be about "seeing," about a hallucinatory vision. Second, in Burke's original version the wilderness that Aschenbach envisions is "prehistoric," but in the revision it is "primeval." The latter word comes from a Latin one for "in the first period of life." It thus connotes something other than just the period before recorded history indicated by "prehistoric," and it better conveys the eras implied by the German word *Urweltwildnis*. Third, the original says that palm trees rise out of a thicket that is "lecherous," whereas the revision describes this thicket as "voluptuous." Again, the latter word comes closer to what Mann says in German. He uses *geil*, an adjective that can indeed mean "lustful" but that means "luxuriant" or "rich" when used to describe plants or soil. The thicket is lush, not lustful, and "voluptuous," which can denote abundance, is more accurate than "lecherous," which more directly has to do with sexual indulgence and which makes no sense when used to describe vegetation. How could a thicket be lecherous? Still, *geil* has strong sexual overtones, not the merely sensual ones audible in "voluptuous." Even the revision therefore falls short. Fourth, in the original, Aschenbach "felt his heart knocking with fear and with puzzling desires," while in the revision he "felt his heart knock with fear and with puzzled desires." In this case, the former wording is better than the latter. There is no difference in meaning here between "knocking" and "knock," and it makes more sense, and is more faithful to Mann, to suggest that the desires are "puzzling," to Aschenbach, than to imply that they themselves are somehow "puzzled." The revision, then, does not always improve the original.

Let us turn now to the translation done by H. T. Lowe-Porter. That translation appeared in London in 1928, then in New York in 1930. It has often been reprinted. Here is how Lowe-Porter renders Aschenbach's vision:

> Desire projected itself visually: his fancy, not quite yet lulled since morning, imaged the marvels and terrors of the manifold earth. He saw. He beheld a landscape, a tropical marshland, beneath a reeking sky, steaming, monstrous, rank—a kind of primeval wilderness-world of islands, morasses, and alluvial channels. Hairy palm-trunks rose near and far out of lush brakes of fern, out of bottoms of crass vegetation, fat, swollen, thick with incredible bloom. There were trees,

mis-shapen as a dream, that dropped their naked roots straight through the air into the ground or into water that was stagnant and shadowy and glassy-green, where mammoth milk-white blossoms floated, and strange high-shouldered birds with curious bills stood gazing sidewise without sound or stir. Among the knotted joints of a bamboo thicket the eyes of a crouching tiger gleamed—and he felt his heart throb with terror, yet with a longing inexplicable.[11]

In some ways, this translation is better than Burke's, but in other ways it is worse, and in many instances it does not correspond to Mann's German. In the introductory lines, "desire" is better than "yearnings," and "the . . . earth" is better than "a . . . world." The word *desire* more clearly implies the sexual appetite connoted by *Begierde*, and "the . . . earth" is the exact equivalent of Mann's "der . . . Erde." Lowe-Porter, however, fails to mention the fact that Aschenbach's imagination is striving—Burke says "struggling"—to picture what he sees. Also, Lowe-Porter's "since morning" does not convey the fact that Aschenbach has been working. In the next several lines, her "steaming" is less accurate than Burke's "damp," she reverses Mann's order of the next two adjectives, and there is no *and* before the last of them, as there should be. In the next part of the passage, she rightly mentions ferns, but she adds an extra adjective, "crass," and she wrongly makes the palm trees the grammatical subject. In Mann's German, that subject is Aschenbach, who is still "seeing." In the next lines, "as in a dream" illogically introduces the idea of dreaming into a scene that is already a vision. There is nothing like this phrase in Mann. Lowe-Porter rightly notes that the trees drop their roots through the air, moreover, but wrongly says that those roots are naked. Mann says nothing of the kind. She also adds "or," incorrectly implying that the ground is separate from the water. Furthermore, she condenses Mann's image of flowers "as large as dishes," as Burke puts it, into a single word: "mammoth." Her "without sound" has no equivalent in Mann, and she neglects to mention that the birds are standing, according to Burke, "in the muck." Finally, she also starts these lines with "There were," rather than with *saw*, as she should. In the next section, she likewise fails to repeat the verb *saw* and thereby to underscore, as Mann does, the fact that Aschenbach envisions all these things. In the final lines of the passage, "inexplicable" is not as close to Mann's "rätselhaftem" as Burke's "puzzling" (or "puzzled"), and "yet" implies that Aschenbach's terror and longing are distinct. Mann uses *und* (and), indicating that these two emotions are of a piece. What is more, Lowe-Porter's punctuation separates this passage into six sentences. In Mann's German, it is only one. In her diction, her choice of words, Lowe-Porter is thus roughly equivalent to Burke. She omits some of what Mann says, however, and she adds some things that he never mentions. In her syntax, the way in which she puts her words together, she fails to convey Mann's repeated reminders that Aschenbach, in his mind's eye and without interruption, "sees."

The next translation of *Death in Venice* into English was done by David Luke. It was published in 1988, sixty years after Lowe-Porter's, just when her copyright expired. Luke's rendering reads as follows:

> . . . turning his craving into vision. His imagination, still not at rest from the morning's hours of work, shaped for itself a paradigm of all the wonders and terrors of the manifold earth, of all that it was now suddenly striving to envisage: he saw it, saw a landscape, a tropical swampland under a cloud-swollen sky, moist and lush and monstrous, a kind of primeval wilderness of islands, morasses and muddy alluvial channels; far and wide around him he saw hairy palm-trunks thrusting upward from rank jungles of fern, from among thick fleshy plants in exuberant flower; saw strangely misshapen trees with roots that arched through the air before sinking into the ground or into stagnant shadowy-green glassy waters where milk-white blossoms floated as big as plates, and among them exotic birds with grotesque beaks stood hunched in the shallows, their heads tilted motionlessly sideways; saw between the knotted stems of the bamboo thicket the glinting eyes of a crouching tiger; and his heart throbbed with terror and mysterious longing.[12]

On the whole, this translation is much better than either Burke's or Lowe-Porter's. It is strange that Luke does not begin the passage with a new sentence, as Mann does. Once he gets started, though, he retains its structure, rhythm, and meaning surprisingly well. His singular "craving" is slightly better than Burke's plural "yearnings," though it may not be as suggestive as Lowe-Porter's "desire." His "at rest" is far closer to Mann's "zur Ruhe gekommen" than either Burke's "still in ferment" or Lowe-Porter's "lulled." His "morning's hours of work" seems to combine the words chosen by Lowe-Porter and by Burke, as does his "muddy alluvial." His "shaped" is not strictly equivalent to Mann's "schuf" (created), but it gives at least some hint of how Aschenbach's imagination works, introducing the phrase "shaped for itself a paradigm." Neither Burke nor Lowe-Porter renders the German equivalent, Mann's "schuf sich ein Beispiel."

By repeating "of all," the next words in the passage, Luke clarifies the antecedents of "that," that is, the words to which this relative pronoun refers. Such additions are sometimes unnecessary, as when he adds "it" after the first instance of "saw," "and" between "moist" and "lush," and "or" when he tells where the trees put down roots. His "cloud-swollen," describing the sky, approximates Mann's "dickdunstigem." When he describes the birds, though, his "hunched" is not the same as "hochschultrig" (high-shouldered), and "their heads tilted" does not equal "blickte" (gazed). Finally, at the end of the passage, where Luke has "his heart throbbed," he neglects to mention that Aschenbach felt it doing so. While a great improvement, then, Luke's translation is far from perfect.

The next English translation appeared in 1994. It was done by Clayton Koelb, and it was published in his Norton Critical Edition of *Death in Venice*. This is the scene in question:

> His desire acquired vision, and his imagination, not yet calmed down from the morning's work, created its own version of the manifold marvels and terrors of the earth, all of them at once now seeking to take shape within him. He saw, saw a landscape, a tropical swamp under a vaporous sky, moist, luxuriant, and monstrous, a sort of primitive wilderness of islands, morasses, and alluvial estuaries; saw hairy palm trunks rise up near and far out of rank fern brakes, out of thick, swollen, wildly blooming vegetation; saw wondrously formless trees sink their aerial roots into the earth through stagnant, green-shadowed pools, where exotic birds, their shoulders high and their bills shaped weirdly, stood motionless in the shallows looking askance amidst floating flowers that were white as milk and big as platters; saw the eyes of a lurking tiger sparkle between the gnarled stems of a bamboo thicket; and felt his heart pound with horror and mysterious desire.[13]

This translation avoids Burke's and Lowe-Porter's major mistakes, and it rectifies some of Luke's minor errors, but also it introduces several new inaccuracies. Like both Lowe-Porter and Luke, Koelb tells when Aschenbach had been working. He does so by using the phrase "morning's work." Mann does not mention the morning here, and Burke's "hours of work" is a better—indeed, a literal—translation of his "Stunden der Arbeit." In Koelb's "created its own version," the word "created" is better than Luke's "shaped," but "its own version" does not render Mann's "ein Beispiel" nearly as well as Luke's "a paradigm." In his "manifold marvels and terrors," Koelb incorrectly uses "manifold" to modify "marvels and terrors" instead of "earth." In "all of them at once now seeking to take shape within him," he wrongly makes those marvels and terrors the grammatical subject. In Mann, the subject is "Einbildungskraft" (imagination), a fact stressing the effort being made by Aschenbach's mind itself. In the second part of the passage, Koelb is the first of the translators studied so far to rightly render Mann's "sah, sah" as "saw, saw." In his description of the sky, "vaporous" conveys the *dunstig,* but not the *dick* (thick) in Mann's composite "dickdunstigem." Calling the trees "wondrously formless" is a good way to translate Mann's "wunderlich ungestalte," though Koelb also says that the trees sink "aerial roots" into the ground. In Mann's German, they sink their roots into the ground "durch die Luft" (through the air). In Koelb's English, those same trees sink their roots "through" pools of water, though Mann uses the preposition *in* (into). In German, these pools are "spiegelnde" (mirroring, reflecting), moreover, a word that Koelb does not relate. What is more, Koelb calls the flowers floating in the pools "white as milk." This phrase parallels the following "big as platters," but there is only one simile in Mann, not two. He writes simply that the flowers were "milchweiß" (milk-white). For that matter, Koelb's "platters" is not equivalent to Mann's "Schüsseln" (dishes, bowls). Koelb also describes the tiger as "lurking," but Mann uses *kauernd* (crouching), a word about the tiger's posture rather than its hiddenness. Finally, at the end of the passage, Koelb's "mysterious" does not convey Mann's word for Aschenbach's longing or desire—"rätselhaftem"—as well as Burke's "puzzling" (or "puzzled"). Compared to the other translations, and especially to Luke's, Koelb's thus seems to lose more than it gains.

In 1995, just a year after Koelb's translation appeared, Stanley Appelbaum's was published in a Dover Thrift Edition. Here is Appelbaum's version of the lines at issue:

> His desire was clairvoyant; his imagination, which had not yet come to rest since his hours of work, summoned up a representative sampling of all the wonders and terrors of the variegated earth, all of which it attempted to visualize at one and the same time: he saw, saw a landscape, a tropical swampy region under a vapor-laden sky, damp, luxuriant and uncanny; it was like the portrait of a primitive world of islands, morasses and silt-laden rivers. From lusty fern clusters, from bottoms in which grew thick, waterlogged plants with outlandish blossoms, he saw hairy palm trunks rising near and far; he saw strangely misshapen trees sinking their roots through the air

into the soil, into stagnant waters that reflected the green shade, where amid floating flowers as white as milk and as large as platters, birds of an exotic species, with hunched shoulders, with monstrous beaks, stood in the shallows and gazed off to the side, motionless; between the knotty, tubular stalks of the bamboo thicket he saw the eyes of a crouching tiger sparkle—and he felt his heart pounding with fright and a puzzling desire.[14]

Appelbaum here renders several words differently than the earlier translators. His new formulations sometimes succeed, but more often than not they fail. In the initial line, his "clairvoyant" makes explicit the extraordinary perceptiveness implicit in Mann's "sehend" (seeing). His "summoned up" is less accurate than Koelb's "created," however, and his "representative sampling" is clumsy. Luke's "paradigm" is better. Used to describe the earth, "variegated" is an alternative to the earlier translators' "manifold." Appelbaum's "at one and the same time" is one equivalent to Mann's "auf einmal," moreover, but is less likely here than Burke's and Luke's "suddenly" or Koelb's nicely ambiguous "at once." Appelbaum's "swampy region" conveys both halves of Mann's composite "Sumpfgebiet," just as his "tubular stalks" renders both halves of Mann's "Rohrstämmen." His "primitive world," however, leaves out the last part, the wilderness, of Mann's "Urweltwildnis." His calling the tropical landscape "uncanny" may make sense, since Mann uses *ungeheuer*, though this word also suggests enormity and monstrousness. There is no equivalent of Appelbaum's "like the portrait" in Mann's German, though, which says "eine Art" (a kind). Furthermore, when used to describe the cluster of ferns, "lusty"— like Burke's initial "lecherous"—does not suggest "fertile" or "luxuriant," two of the meanings of *geil*. Likewise, Appelbaum says that the plants are "waterlogged, " unduly shifting the emphasis of Mann's "gequollen," the past participle of *quellen* (flow, swell). The plants are swollen, not soggy. Similarly, when he calls the blossoms on those plants "outlandish," he introduces the idea of foreignness, otherwise so important in *Death in Venice*, where Mann does not. The adverb Mann uses here is *abenteuerlich* (adventurously, unusually). With "into the soil, into the . . . waters," Appelbaum is the first translator since Burke to get this apposition right. Like Koelb, though, he writes that the flowers are "as white as milk," introducing a comparison not found in Mann's German. "Monstrous," the word he chooses to describe the birds' beaks, closely corresponds to Mann's "unförmig." Finally, Appelbaum always adds "he" before "saw." After the first occurrence of "sah," however, Mann repeats the verb only. Like

Burke, he also splits Mann's single, long sentence into two shorter ones. Appelbaum, then, seems to cause more problems than he solves.

Yet another English translation appeared three years later, in 1998. It is the work of Joachim Neugroschel, who renders the passage like this:

> His desire could virtually see, his ability to fantasize, unlulled since his hours of working, conjured up all the wonders and terrors, all the variety of the earth, which he strove to envision. He saw, saw a landscape, a tropical quagmire under a steamy sky, muggy, luxuriant, and monstrous, a primordial jungle of islands, morasses, and alluvial inlets; saw hairy palm shafts near and far striving upward out of rank and rampant ferns, realms of fat, swollen plants with fantastic blossoms; saw eccentrically misshapen trees plunging their roots through the air and into the ground, into stagnant waters reflecting green shadows; saw bowl-sized, milky white flowers drifting on surfaces and outlandish species of birds, with hunched shoulders and deformed beaks, standing in shallow liquids and inertly ogling sideways; saw the sparkling eyes of a crouching tiger between the knotty canes of the bamboo thicket—and he felt his heart pounding with horror and enigmatic longing.[15]

Like Appelbaum, Neugroschel renders many of Mann's words differently than the four earlier translators. Unlike Appelbaum, he usually does so successfully. He is especially good at conveying the etymological roots of those words, though his English sometimes seems too suggestive. In "could virtually see," "see" captures the root of Mann's "sehend" (seeing), but "virtually" spells out what is merely implicit in Mann, who uses *sehend* by itself, and "could" does not stress the act or process of acquiring vision. Mann's archaic "ward" does. Neugroschel loses this same distinction in "which he strove to envision." The verb "strove" is good insofar as it corresponds to the root of *bestrebt* in Mann's "bestrebt war," but *was striving*, the progressive aspect of this past-tense verb, would be better. He correctly captures this same root, which Mann repeats, when he describes the palms as "striving upward." He wrongly suggests a similar link, however, when he mentions Aschenbach's "ability to fantasize," then calls the blossoms "fantastic." Mann forges no such link with his two unrelated words, "Einbildungskraft" (imagination) and "abenteuerlich" (adventurously, unusually). In the rest of Neugroschel's first sentence, "unlulled" is an unfortunate echo of Lowe-Porter's "lulled"; "conjured up" shifts the emphasis of "schuf" (created); "all the variety of the earth" differs from

Mann's wording, which most of the other translators render when they call the earth itself "manifold" or "variegated"; and there is no indication at all that Aschenbach envisions this scene "auf einmal" (at once). In Neugroschel's second sentence—like Burke and Appelbaum, he has two in place of Mann's one—there is a similar alternation of apt and over-reaching words. "Primordial jungle," "inlets," "reflecting green shadows," "deformed," and "enigmatic longing" are all good equivalents of the German words Mann uses to describe the setting, the birds' beaks, and Aschenbach's mixed emotions. "Eccentrically," "drifting," and "outlandish" are also acceptable, given the ones he uses for the trees, flowers, and birds. Like Luke and Appelbaum, Neugroschel calls the birds "hunched," a word less strictly accurate than the other translators' "high-shouldered." "Shallow liquids" is awkward, since it implies, though Mann does not, that there are liquids other than water in the swamp. Both "quagmire" and "ogling" are too suggestive. Figuratively, the former denotes a difficult situation. Mann's "Sumpfgebiet" (swampy region) does not. The latter suggests staring that is impertinent or amorous, and though this sort of staring often occurs in Mann's story, it is not what the birds are doing here. Whereas Koelb and Appelbaum add a simile not found in Mann's German when they call the flowers "white as milk," moreover, Neugroschel subtracts one when he calls those flowers "bowl-sized." Mann writes "groß wie Schüsseln" (big as bowls). Neugroschel hints at the sound of Mann's prose, however, with the initial r in "rank," "rampant," and "realms." Mann achieves similar alliteration with the initial g in his "geil" and "Gründen." Neugroschel is thus subtle, though he sometimes tends to overinterpret what he translates.

The most recent English translation of *Death in Venice* is by Jefferson S. Chase. It was published in 1999, and it includes this equivalent of the passage in question:

> Craving had gained the power of sight, and his imagination, which had still not calmed down after his hours of hard work, was creating for itself a single emblematic scene, laboring to picture all the wonders and terrors of the multifarious world at one and the same time. He saw . . . saw a landscape, a tropical swamp under a sky thick with vapor, damp, lush and monstrous, a kind of primeval wilderness of islands, bogs and sediment-carrying channels . . . saw hairy trunks of palm trees pushing up near and far from fecund tangles of ferns and beds of oily, swollen, outlandishly blooming flora . . . saw bizarrely deformed trees with roots growing down through the air

into the earth, into the green shadows reflected in sluggish flood-waters where, between floating, milky-white flowers the size of plates, birds of some alien species stood in the shadows with hunched shoulders and clumsily shaped beaks and stared immovably off to one side . . . saw through the knotted shoots of a bamboo thicket the glint from the eyes of a crouching tiger . . . and felt his heart pound with horror and inexplicable longing.[16]

Chase here translates some words better than others. In his initial lines, he alters three of Mann's verbs. "Had gained the power of sight" is in the wrong tense. Mann's "ward" (became) is in the imperfect, not the pluperfect. "Had still not calmed down" is likewise in the pluperfect, but there is no equivalent of "had" in Mann's German. This auxiliary verb could be construed as implicit, though, so it is acceptable. "Was creating" conveys the wrong aspect of Mann's "schuf" (created). Chase also adds an adjective when he says that Aschenbach's work was "hard." Likewise, "single" does not come from Mann, though "emblematic scene" is an adequate rendering of "Beispiel." "Laboring" is not equivalent to Mann's "bestrebt," and though "multifarious" works, "world" is awkward, since Chase uses it for "Erde" (earth) here, then later uses "earth" for "Boden" (ground). "At one and the same time," as in Appelbaum, does not do justice to Mann's "auf einmal," which also means "suddenly." In the rest of the passage as well, Chase is sometimes accurate but sometimes off the mark. "Thick with vapor" is an excellent translation of "dickdunstigem"; "sediment-carrying" is equivalent to Mann's "Schlamm führenden"; "fecund," "oily," and "flora" are nice new twists on "geil," "fett," and "Pflanzenwerk"; and "bizarrely deformed" is fine for describing the trees. One could quibble that "with roots growing down" does not fully account for those trees' sinking or plunging their roots into the ground, and it is not entirely accurate to say that the roots extend "into the green shadows reflected in sluggish flood waters." In German, the roots go into the water reflecting the shadows, not the shadows themselves. "Of some alien species," "clumsily shaped," and "stared immovably" are all good choices in the description of the birds. Here, too, those birds are "hunched" instead of high-shouldered, though, and it is incorrect to say that they stood "in the shadows." Mann's writes "im Seichten," and perhaps Chase's phrase is a mistranslation or a misprint of its equivalent: "in the shallows." The ellipses before all but the first "saw" are not in Mann's German, which has commas there, plus a dash before the third. These series of periods, though, make the structure of the passage plain by heralding each repetition of this crucial verb. Finally—like Burke, Appelbaum, and Neugroschel—Chase splits the passage into two sentences. In sum, Chase translates in ways that are sometimes new but that are also often no better and that are occasionally worse than those of his six predecessors.

Which of these several translations is best? The answer to that question depends on what one needs and wants. As noted above, each has its strengths and weaknesses. There are also other factors to consider. Some translations contain *Death in Venice* only; others include selections from Mann's other writings. Some come with an introduction, background information, and a sampling of secondary literature; others do not include any, or have some but not all, of these supplementary items. Here are the main features of each:

When published as a book in 1925, Burke's translation of 1924 appeared together with two of Mann's prior stories, *Tristan* and *Tonio Kröger*. Appended to the revision of 1970 is an essay by Erich Heller, *Autobiography and Literature*. The revision also includes a biographical table of the main dates and events in Mann's life, as well as a list of American editions of Mann's principal works published by Alfred A. Knopf in New York. In 1972, the Stinehour Press published the revision in a limited edition illustrated by Felix Hoffmann.

In 1930, the first American edition of Lowe-Porter's translation of 1928 included an introduction by Ludwig Lewisohn. Since then, that translation has appeared along with her renderings of other stories by Mann. He wrote some of those stories before, and some of them after, *Death in Venice*.

Luke's translation of 1988 appeared together with his versions of six of Mann's other, earlier stories. His long introduction ends with an analysis of Lowe-Porter's most egregious mistakes. This translation is also included in editions prepared by Naomi Ritter in 1998 and by Frederick A. Lubich in 1999.[17] Ritter's contains her own introduction to Mann's biography and historical contexts; her history of the reception of *Death in Venice*; and five essays, by as many scholars, that either treat various issues it raises or take various critical approaches to it. The topics of those essays are history and community (Russell A. Berman), cultural multiplicity (John Burt Foster, Jr.), the potential deceptiveness of reading (Lilian R. Furst), psychoanalytic approaches (Rodney Symington), and a gay perspective (Robert Tobin). Ritter's edition also contains a glossary of critical and theoretical terms. Lubich's edition includes five of Mann's other stories and three of his essays, most translated by Luke or Lowe-Porter, as well as Lubich's introduction and a foreword by Harold Bloom.

Koelb's translation of 1994 includes footnotes and is followed by two supplementary sections. The section entitled "Backgrounds and Contexts" contains maps of Munich in 1910 and of Venice and the Lido around 1911, as well as English translations, done by Lynda Hoffman Jeep, of Mann's working notes for *Death in Venice* and of extracts from letters and essays in which he mentions that novella or raises topics related to it. The section entitled "Criticism" contains six essays, by various scholars, on Mann's combination of "myth plus psychology" (André von Gronicka); on the influence of Nietzsche's *Birth of Tragedy* (Manfred Dierks); on Mann's "art of ambivalence" (T. J. Reed); on his "second author," his narrator (Dorrit Cohn); on his "iridescent interweaving" of conflicting elements (David Luke); and on perspectives on homoeroticism (Robert Tobin). Koelb, the editor as well as the translator, also provides a chronology of Mann's life, not to mention a selected bibliography of secondary literature.

Appelbaum's translation of 1995 includes a brief history of the genesis of *Death in Venice*, an afterword about translating it, and a commentary that treats the year—1911—in which the fictional events of the novella occur, the real-life models for Aschenbach, his career, the topography of the novella, the Polish names that Mann mentions, Mann's leitmotifs and symbolism, his classical references, and his miscellaneous allusions, as well as his phrases in French.

Neugroschel's translation of 1998 contains a translator's preface and his renderings of eleven of Mann's other, earlier stories.

Chase's translation of 1999 begins with an introduction and ends with suggestions for further reading. It is published along with Chase's translations of six of Mann's other stories, five of them written before *Death in Venice* and one written after it.

Of these eight translations (counting the revision of Burke's separately), then, Burke's and Lowe-Porter's are the oldest—and thus the ones most often cited in the secondary literature that relies on an English rendering of *Death in Venice*; Luke's is the one most frequently included in editions or in anthologies prepared by someone other than the translator; Koelb's provides the largest amount and range of supplementary material; Appelbaum's is the least expensive; Neugroschel's has the widest selection of Mann's other fiction; and Chase's is the most recent. It is also striking how widely the number of words used in these translations differs. In the passage just considered, that number ranges from a minimum of 151 (Lowe-Porter) to a maximum of 190 (Appelbaum). The average is about 171. Mann used only 149 in German.

NOTES

1. Translated by Lynda Hoffman Jeep in *Death in Venice*, trans. and ed. Clayton Koelb (New York: Norton, 1994), 92.

2. Ibid., 93.

3. Ibid.

4. Ibid.

5. Ibid.

6. Ibid.

7. This judgment, the reason for it, and the analysis of the particular passage cited here come from Terence James Reed, "Der falsche Text des *Tod in Venedig*, oder: wie ist ein Meistersatz zu retten?", *Thomas Mann Jahrbuch* 9 (1996), 293–302.

8. *Der Tod in Venedig*, ed. A. W. Hornsey (Boston: Houghton Mifflin, 1969); *Der Tod in Venedig*, ed. T. J. Reed (Oxford: Oxford University Press, 1971); *Der Tod in Venedig*, ed. George E. Boyd and Henry M. Rosenwald (New York: Oxford University Press, 1973).

9. *Death in Venice*, trans. Kenneth Burke, quoted in *Great German Short Novels and Stories*, ed. Victor Lange (New York: Modern Library, 1952), 404.

10. *Death in Venice*, trans. Kenneth Burke (New York: Modern Library, 1970), 6–7.

11. *Death in Venice and Seven Other Stories*, trans. H. T. Lowe-Porter (New York: Vintage, 1954), 5–6.

12. *Death in Venice and Other Stories*, trans. David Luke (New York: Bantam, 1988), 197.

13. *Death in Venice*, trans. and ed. Clayton Koelb (New York: Norton, 1994), 5.

14. *Death in Venice*, trans. Stanley Appelbaum (New York: Dover, 1995), 3.

15. *Death in Venice and Other Tales*, trans. Joachim Neugroschel (New York: Penguin, 1998), 290.

16. *Death in Venice and Other Stories*, trans. Jefferson S. Chase (New York: Signet, 1999), 141–42.

17. *Death in Venice*, ed. Naomi Ritter (Boston: Bedford, 1998); *Death in Venice, Tonio Kröger, and Other Writings*, ed. Frederick A. Lubich (New York: Continuum, 1999).

4   Contexts

The text of *Death in Venice* reflects a broader context: the international situation and the intellectual environment in which Mann wrote it. This context consists of the historical, cultural, and sociological factors that figure in his story, as well as of many literary and other influences that affected him more or less directly. Those historical factors include both the political prelude to the First World War and the militaristic career of Frederick the Great. Among those cultural and sociological factors are the idea of Prussianism, as analyzed by the critic Georg Lukács; Protestantism, as explained by the sociologist Max Weber; and modernism, as studied by the author Samuel Lublinski. The most important literary influences come from modern Germany and France or ancient Greece. They are treatises, poems, novels, a letter, epics, and dialogues by Friedrich Schiller, August von Platen, Johann Wolfgang von Goethe, Gustave Flaubert, Homer, Xenophon, Plutarch, or Plato. Among the other influences are writings by the classical philologist Erwin Rohde, by the philosopher Arthur Schopenhauer, and, again, by Lukács. Like the historical, cultural, and sociological factors that contribute to Mann's story, these literary or other influences date not only from the late nineteenth or early twentieth centuries, then, but also from the eighteenth, or even from antiquity. Mann's novella addresses issues that preceded it, therefore, by over a hundred years in Germany and by over two thousand in Greece.

HISTORICAL, CULTURAL, AND SOCIOLOGICAL FACTORS

The First World War and Frederick the Great

Mann hints at the historical background of his story in its very first sentence. He there explains that it is the year "19..., das unserem Kontinent eine so gefahrdrohende Miene zeigte" (19..., which displayed to our continent such a threatening mien). "Our continent" is Europe, and the threat to which Mann here alludes is usually inferred to be one of the diplomatic crises that preceded the First World War, perhaps the second Moroccan crisis. This international incident occurred in 1911, when Germany sent the cruiser *Panther* to Agadir, a port town on the Atlantic coast of Morocco. A similar, first Moroccan crisis had taken place in 1905. Both involved German objections to plans to establish a French protectorate there. As a result of the second, Germany received part of French Equatorial Africa in present-day Cameroon. These crises show the effects of the foreign policy pursued by Wilhelminian Germany—the German Empire between 1890 and 1914, when it was ruled by Wilhelm II, who ascended the throne in 1888 and abdicated at the end of the First World War in 1918.[1] That policy called for establishing overseas colonies and for building a naval fleet to rival those of England and France. It led to international tensions and seems to have been meant to defuse German domestic conflicts. Those conflicts resulted from attempts to maintain the political dominance of conservative Prussia in a Germany that was both enjoying the economic prosperity and undergoing the social upheavals that came with its rapid industrialization. Prussia was the largest, but hardly the only, state in Germany then. Among those upheavals was the internal emigration of workers from east to west, and the population in several eastern regions of Prussia was mostly Polish. Furthermore, in 1906, Phillip zu Eulenburg (1847–1921), one of Wilhelm's closest advisors, was publicly, and perhaps falsely, accused by the publicist Maximilan Harden (1861–1927) of homosexuality, a criminal offense at the time. Wilhelminian Germany thus was marked by adventures abroad that distracted its attention from conflicts at home, by encounters with the East, especially with Poles, and by a prominent scandal involving homosexuality. In these three respects, Germany may seem like Aschenbach, who would then appear to embody its general historical trends. Mann suggests some such historical parallel by indicating that his hero, like Europe, is somehow endangered. At this early point in his story, though, that parallel seems to be broadly European, not specifically German. All of Europe, that is, seems threatened.

Another indication that the fictional events of *Death in Venice* have to do with the First World War is Mann's description of Aschenbach's trip to Venice in chapter 3. That description includes two notable expressions. First, Mann describes Pola, a port in southern Istria, a peninsula on the Adriatic, as a "Kriegshafen" (war harbor, naval base). At the time Mann was writing his story, this city belonged to Austria-Hungary. Indeed, it had been an Austrian possession since 1797. Before that, it had belonged to Venice. It became part of Italy in 1919, after the defeat of Austria and Germany. Its military status thus suggests the ethnic conflicts that occasioned both Balkan Wars of 1912–1913 as well as the First World War itself, which began when archduke Francis Ferdinand of Austria-Hungary was assassinated by a Serbian nationalist in Sarajevo on 28 June 1914. Sarajevo was the capital of Bosnia-Herzegovina, a Balkan province that Austria annexed in 1908. Second, as Aschenbach's ship approaches Venice, Mann mentions that the clerks from Pola are patriotically attracted by military horn signals coming from the area around its public gardens and that they cheer the *bersaglieri* drilling there. These sharpshooters are in the service of Italy, a country unified as recently as 1861. It has included Venice only since 1866. Prior to that, Venice, like Pola, had belonged to Austria since 1797. The tipsy clerks thus cheer the political example set by Venice, a city no longer subject to Austria. Even more clearly than the unspecified threat to Europe posed by the year "19…", then, Aschenbach's trip from Pola to Venice suggests that his story is set in a highly charged historical situation. By using the words *Kriegshafen* and *bersaglieri*, that is, Mann hints at tensions between Austria and its subjects in southeastern Europe. Aschenbach comes from Germany, of course, not Austria. Nonetheless, such prewar tensions seem part of his life. He, too, confronts people from the southern and eastern regions of "our continent."

Further geopolitical conclusions and distinctions can be drawn from Mann's use of other revealing terms. All of those terms are tied to Frederick the Great (1712–86), the king of Prussia from 1740 until his death. In chapter 2, Mann notes that Frederick is the subject of one of Aschenbach's works. He also observes that Aschenbach was born in "L," a city in Silesia. As noted earlier, Silesia is a province that currently lies mostly in Poland. Mann's working notes suggest that "L" stands for Liegnitz (or Legnica, as it is known in Polish). The history of this city seems linked to Aschenbach's story. In 1241, the Mongols defeated a Polish army there. Five hundred years later, in 1741, Liegnitz passed from the Habsburgs, the ruling family of Austria, to Prussia, and in 1760 it was the site of one of Frederick's military victories over Austria in the Seven

Years' War (1756–63). It thus is a place where Europeans succumbed to an enemy from Asia and where Prussia would have defeated Aschenbach's ancestors, had they actually existed. Mann alludes to the latter, fictional fact, again in chapter 2, when he says that Aschenbach writes with the same tenacity and toughness that conquered his native province. Aschenbach has thus assumed characteristics of Frederick, military qualities that are foreign to him. Finally, in chapter 3, Mann notes that Tadzio looks scornfully at the good-natured Russian family, his enemies. This seemingly unprovoked behavior reflects the fact that Poland, at the time Mann described that behavior, had long been subject to the cultural influence and political dominance of Russia. Poland was subject to both such influence and such dominance from Prussia and Austria as well, a fact dating from 1772, the year in which these three countries first partitioned it. That was during Frederick's reign. In 1792 and 1795, after he died, a second and third partition of Poland ensued. As a result, Poland disappeared off the map of Europe until after the First World War. The political circumstances obtaining in Mann's novella arose in part, then, from Frederick's military and diplomatic conquests. When put in this historical perspective, those circumstances suggest that Europe, or at least Aschenbach, is threatened from the east and west alike.

These allusions and references to Frederick the Great, as well as other connections one can draw between him and Aschenbach, show how carefully one needs to consider German history and geography before judging Mann's story. Aschenbach is not simply German, nor is he entirely Prussian. He is Silesian, and though he has taken on traits of the Prussian king who initiated a historical process that eventually led to the unification of Germany in 1871, he lives in Bavaria, which retained certain privileges of a sovereign state then. The pronounced historical and cultural differences between these regions of Germany as it existed at the time Mann wrote *Death in Venice*, not to mention the armed conflicts that had occurred between them, make his hero complex. Aschenbach is from an eastern province, a region near—and historically, at times, part of—Poland. He resides in Munich, moreover, a southern German, artistic capital that differs markedly from the more northern Berlin or Potsdam, in Brandenburg, where Frederick's family lived. Even his similarity to Frederick is complicated, for the Prussian king was far more than just a military man. Throughout his life, Frederick cultivated his serious musical, literary, and artistic interests. He also resembles Aschenbach in several ways.[2] As a result of his often brutal upbringing, he almost always submitted his emotions to reason. He showed self-control to the point of asceticism, suppressed his sensuality, and succeeded by the force of his will and his strong sense of duty. He was ambitious, stoic, and disciplined, but he was not robust, and by the end of the Seven Years' War in 1763, he had just turned fifty-one and was exhausted. Finally, he died without family or friends. In all these ways, he is similar to Aschenbach. The conquest of Silesia in the War of the Austrian Succession (1740–48), however, and its retention as a result of the Seven Years' War, were the focus of Frederick's military and political career, a feat that established Prussia as a European power. In the essay *Friedrich und die große Koalition* (Frederick and the Grand Coalition, 1915), moreover, Mann notes that Frederick was deeply misogynistic and that his manliness appears not to have been attracted to its female opposite in the usual way. Indeed, the Prussian monarch whose habits of mind Aschenbach emulates was often alleged, perhaps falsely, to have been homosexual.[3]

Prussianism, Protestantism, Modernism

A further, ethical link between Aschenbach and Frederick's Prussia was drawn by the Hungarian literary critic Georg Lukács (1885–1971). In an essay titled *Auf der Suche nach dem Bürger* (In Search of Bourgeois Man, 1945), Lukács argues that *Tonio Kröger* (1903) and *Death in Venice* display Mann's characteristic dilemma of composure and emotional anarchy. Can an artistic career, he asks, can any kind of genuine culture, result from composure, from restraining the emotions? The first novella seems to show that such composure is the ethic of the bourgeoisie, Lukács maintains, but Mann judges himself ruthlessly in the second. Aschenbach's life and work are based on an ethic of composure, he explains, but a minor conflict and a dream are all it takes to make that composure break down. This ethic, Lukács says, is also intimately connected with the finest intellectual figures in Wilhelminian Germany. They, too, in his opinion, typically had to choose between emotional anarchy and composure. What is more, Mann's own development shows how that ethic leads to Prussianism. It is no accident, he explains, that Aschenbach has written an epic about Frederick the Great, a work foreshadowing the essay that Mann wrote about Frederick in the First World War. Yet Mann has also exposed the ethic of composure as worthless and unreal, Lukács writes, has unmasked the inner weakness of Prussianized behavior. Lukács made similar arguments elsewhere. In *Die Tragödie der modernen Kunst* (The Tragedy of Modern Art, 1949), he adds that *Death in Venice* is anticipatory criticism of Mann's patriotic writings during the First World War. In *Das Spielerische*

und seine Hintergründe (The Playful Style, 1955), he thinks that
Aschenbach's grotesque tragedy and degrading death display Mann's skepticism toward bourgeois society and appear to defy the noble stoicism for
which Aschenbach has stood. *Death in Venice*, he also observes, points
beyond the conflict between artists and the bourgeoisie. It shows that the
function of art in bourgeois society is inevitably paradoxical, but also
"points to the problem of action in our time." In its self-contained and
concentrated form, the literary form of a novella, however, Mann "indicates more the social, psychological and moral premises and consequences
than action itself."[4] In such general claims, Lukács sounds vague, but his
main point is clear: *Death in Venice* exposes the hollow Prussian ethic of
Wilhelminian Germany.

In his remarks on bourgeois culture prior to the First World War, remarks made in the essay *In Search of Bourgeois Man*, Lukács notes that
leading sociologists tried to "Aschenbachize"[5] the middle class's quest for
wealth. He seems to mean that these sociologists lent that quest moral
and sociocultural legitimacy. At any rate, one of the sociologists he names
is Max Weber (1864–1920), and Aschenbach's significance can be explained in terms taken from Weber's *Die protestantische Ethik und der Geist
des Kapitalismus* (The Protestant Ethic and the Spirit of Capitalism), a
book first published as an article in 1904–5, eight years before *Death in
Venice*. Weber's argument posits a close relationship between religious
beliefs and economic behavior. Protestant asceticism, according to him,
laid the ethical basis of modern capitalism, for the rational acquisition of
wealth. This is especially clear in Calvinism, Weber remarks, which made
the legal pursuit of monetary profit seem morally justified, even ethically
obligatory. To follow this argument, one needs to know the terms that
Weber employs. *Asceticism* is extreme self-discipline, especially when prac-
ticed from religious motives. *Capitalism* is the economic system based on
free markets and the private and corporate ownership of business enter-
prises operated for profit. *Calvinism* comprises theological doctrines set
forth by John Calvin (1509–64). Those doctrines included predestina-
tion—the doctrine that all things are foreordained by God—and redemption by God's grace alone. The link between these terms is the concept
of the calling. A *calling* is a vocation, a professional occupation. As Weber
explains, Calvinism regarded success in a worldly calling as a sign, though
not a means, of one's salvation. One pursues such activity, that is, to prove
one's faith and to assure oneself of future redemption. This requires rational planning of practical life, including economic conduct. The idea
of duty in a calling thus relates the ethics of Protestant asceticism and

the spirit of capitalism. As Weber himself expresses this thought, "The religious valuation of restless, continuous, systematic work in a worldly calling, as the highest means to asceticism, and at the same time the surest and most evident proof of rebirth and genuine faith, must have been the most powerful conceivable lever for the expansion of that attitude toward life which we have . . . called the spirit of capitalism."[6] Weber does not hold that the Protestant Reformation created or caused capitalism, only that it formed and expanded it. He also maintains that the ethic of discipline in a calling lost its religious sense and became utilitarian. As an example of its secular application, he cites the business-minded advice given by Benjamin Franklin.

What do Weber's remarks about the connection between religion and economics have to do with *Death in Venice*? Aschenbach is neither pious nor a capitalist, of course, but he is both ascetic and affluent, having gained worldly success by dint of hard work. In Mann's second chapter, he also is said to speak for fellow "Moralisten der Leistung" (moralists of achievement), the weak and exhausted heroes of his age. The relevance of Weber's concepts to Mann's story thus seems to be social as well as psychological. Both Aschenbach's self-discipline and his representative role, that is, seem related to Weber's ideas. Like the Calvinists and capitalists whom Weber studies, Aschenbach controls his emotions and has not indulged in any spontaneous enjoyment of life. In his society, that of Wilhelminian Germany, moreover, his strict work ethic had economic consequences. Aschenbach's industry, one might say, is tied to German industrialization. One might also note that Weber, like Lukács, writes about the ethics of the bourgeoisie. Weber's focus is not limited to Germany, however, or to the nineteenth or early twentieth century. Instead, it includes several Western European countries, and it regards them since the Protestant Reformation in the sixteenth. His study thus suggests further ways in which "our continent"—as Mann says, in German—of Europe is threatened.

Another sociological study that helps shed light on *Death in Venice* appeared in the same year as Weber's and is titled *Die Bilanz der Moderne* (A Survey of Modernism, 1904). It is by Samuel Lublinski (1868–1910), an author who wrote on various subjects, and it is about German literature since roughly 1885. Lublinski criticizes naturalism as well as neoromanticism, two literary trends and styles found in German plays, poems, and prose fiction then. He comments on *Buddenbrooks* (1901), Mann's first novel, which tells how a northern German merchant family declines, and he calls its author the most significant modern novelist in Germany.

Mann, he adds, describes social circumstances with naturalistic objectivity, which involves an intellectual and youthful manliness that bites its teeth in proud shame and that stands calmly while swords and spears pierce its body. This attitude corresponds, Lublinski contends, to the character of Mann's fictional figures. *Buddenbrooks* is the first and only naturalistic novel in Germany, he maintains, and, like naturalism in general, it leaves no room for the personality, that is, for an active individual will. It describes passive heroism, though, he says, in a way that can hardly be outdone. These observations about *Buddenbrooks* pertain to *Death in Venice* because Mann quotes one of them. In his second chapter, he writes that a smart "analyst" once noted how Aschenbach's fictional heroes are the embodiment of "einer intellektuellen und jünglinghaften Männlichkeit . . . die in stolzer Scham die Zähne aufeinanderbeißt und ruhig dasteht, während ihr die Schwerter und Speere durch den Leib gehen." In German, these are the words Lublinski uses when he praises the style and the heroism of *Buddenbrooks*. Mann applies these words to Aschenbach, perhaps suggesting that his hero's kind of writing and characters are like what his own had been ten years before he started *Death in Venice* in 1911. According to Lublinski, moreover, bourgeois authors could not understand the new world of the working class. Aschenbach might thus also seem to be such an author, one whose grasp of that workaday world is limited. In a subsequent book, *Der Ausgang der Moderne* (The End of Modernism, 1909), Lublinski qualifies his praise of *Buddenbrooks*, which he now regards as a psychological and individualistic novel, less than a social one. He also calls for a modern classicality. Mann may expose such neoclassicism by having Aschenbach take it too far, although Mann himself was attracted to it, thanks to Lublinski.[7] Reading *Death in Venice* in light of Lublinski's sociological-literary insights in any case suggests that Aschenbach and the kind of fiction he writes seem out of step with modern times.

LITERARY AND OTHER INFLUENCES

Like the historical, cultural, and sociological factors just cited, literary and other influences helped shape *Death in Venice*. Those influences included eleven ancient and modern authors. Mann seldom explicitly refers to these authors or their writings. More often, he only implicitly alludes to them, quoting or paraphrasing them without giving their names or citing the titles of their works. Sometimes, an author's influence on his novella can be discerned from remarks he made in notes, letters, essays, or interviews. Regardless of how or where he mentions such influences or how directly they affected him, they suggest the context of his story in ways that can help clarify its significance.

Literary Influences: Modern Germany and France

The list of Aschenbach's works given at the beginning of Mann's second chapter includes an aesthetic treatise, *Geist und Kunst* (Intellect and Art). The ordering force and antithetical eloquence of this treatise, Mann observes, had led serious readers to place it "unmittelbar neben Schillers Raisonnement über naive und sentimentalische Dichtung" (immediately next to Schiller's *raisonnement* on naive and sentimental poetry). This is a reference to the author Friedrich Schiller (1759–1805), who wrote the "Ode to Joy" sung in the last movement of Beethoven's Ninth Symphony. The word *raisonnement*, being French, stands out in Mann's German no less than it does in English. It denotes rational argument or analytical observations, and Mann uses it here to describe Schiller's essay *Über naive und sentimentalische Dichtung* (On Naive and Sentimental Poetry, 1795–96). In Schiller's sense, a "naive" poet is in harmony with nature, realistic, and spontaneous. By contrast, a "sentimental" poet is alienated from nature, idealistic, and reflective. Such a modern poet is aware of his alienation and wishes to overcome it, to return to nature, albeit by means of reason and free will. Schiller's remarks are more complex than this seemingly simple opposition suggests. It is possible, though, to regard Aschenbach in these terms. He could be called "sentimental," that is, an author who once felt cut off from nature and who has striven to be reunited with it. Mann's second chapter recalls, in fact, that he has since undergone a "Wunder der wiedergeborenen Unbefangenheit" (miracle of reborn naiveté). Aschenbach might thus seem to have reconciled his senses and his intellect in the way that Schiller posits. His story appears to end badly for him, moreover, which may seem to cast doubt on this synthesis. This reference to Schiller would then pertain not only to the logic and the style of Aschenbach's prose, but also to the tragic course of his literary career.

Aschenbach can also be understood according to some of Schiller's other works. He can be seen in the equally antithetical terms of another of Schiller's aesthetic essays, for example, *Über Anmut und Würde* (On Grace and Dignity, 1793). This essay contrasts inclination and duty. In a beautiful soul, expressed in "grace," these concepts coincide. In most people, though, they are at odds, and people who do their moral duty, despite contrary inclinations, show "dignity." Again, Schiller's argument is more complex than the apparently simple contrast of such terms suggests. As stated earlier, though, Mann often mentioned the idea of artists' dignity in letters that explain what he meant to say in *Death in Venice*. One of his working notes likewise mentions Aschenbach's ascent to dignity. Mann knew his Schiller, moreover, so it seems legitimate to interpret his hero's struggle to attain—and then to preserve—dignity as an effort to will what is rational in spite of what is sensual. This is how Schiller defines dignity, and it is what Aschenbach, in the end, fails to do. Again, Mann's hero appears to fall short of Schiller's ideal. In any event, Schiller here relates art to ethics, as he also does in another of his essays, *Über die ästhetische Erziehung des Menschen* (On the Aesthetic Education of Man, 1795). This essay holds that art can be educational because it refines human sensibilities. Beauty, in other words, can have a moral effect because it links sensuality to reason, links the physical to the intellectual. Yet again, Schiller's reasoning is far more intricate than such a summary of his ideas suggests, and yet again Aschenbach's story seems to contradict those ideas. Aschenbach himself, in Mann's final chapter, concludes that artists' sensuality prevents them from ever becoming truly wise and dignified. Along the path of beauty, he thinks, artists are accosted by Eros, by passion and desire. Educating people by means of art is therefore risky, he muses, and should be forbidden. Aschenbach thus seems to reject the entire notion of aesthetic education that was so important to Schiller. Finally, Schiller is the protagonist of Mann's *Schwere Stunde* (A Difficult Hour, 1905), and in this story, he, like Aschenbach, has two candles "zu Häupten des Manuskripts" (at the head of his manuscript). That Mann uses this phrase while describing both authors' monastic work habits is a further sign that *Death in Venice* has to do with Schiller.

Another German author who figures in the novella is the poet August von Platen (1796–1835). Unlike Schiller, he is not mentioned by name. Mann instead merely alludes to his *Sonette aus Venedig* (Sonnets from Venice, 1825). Mann does so in chapter 3, when Aschenbach thinks of a poet who preceded him to Venice and silently recites to himself some of that poet's verse. Platen traveled to Venice half a dozen times, starting in 1824. The sonnets he wrote on his first trip tell of the places, people, and works of art that he saw there. They also reflect on the rise and fall of Venice, a city with a glorious past but little present vitality, as well as on beauty in art and life and on unrequited love. Platen was homosexual, so when Aschenbach is moved by feelings that Platen articulated and wonders if an emotional adventure awaits him, too, he may have a homosexual love in mind. In any case, Platen is in some ways like Aschenbach. Long a resident of Munich, for example, he combined poetic talent with his military training. Aschenbach, at home in Munich, is never actually a soldier, but he does prefer to think of himself as one. Like Aschenbach's prose, moreover, Platen's poems display great formal polish. Platen died in Syracuse, Sicily, furthermore, wrongly assuming that he had contracted cholera. Like Schiller, then, Platen is an author whose life and whose works seem folded into those of Mann's fictional hero.

A third such German author is Johann Wolfgang von Goethe (1749–1832). Mann, as noted earlier, wrote several letters in which he claims that he had originally intended *Death in Venice* to be about how the aging Goethe lost his dignity by falling in love with Ulrike von Levetzow (1804–99), a young woman more than fifty years his junior. Mann never executed this supposed plan, though his novella can indeed be read as showing a conflict between intellect and life, a conflict that he claimed he had intended to describe by using this episode from Goethe's biography. Mann also remarked on more than one occasion that he repeatedly read Goethe's *Die Wahlverwandtschaften* (Elective Affinities, 1809) while writing *Death in Venice*. Goethe there relates an erotic tragedy, telling how Eduard and Charlotte, a married couple, are attracted to Ottilie, Charlotte's niece, and to a captain, Eduard's friend, respectively. His novel, then, is about tension between natural passions and moral order, between necessity and freedom. It turns out badly for its main characters, ending in frustrated desire, renouncement, and death. It therefore seems similar to Mann's novella, and the two stories have often been compared. *Death in Venice* also recalls Goethe's *Der Mann von funfzig Jahren* (A Man of Fifty), a story within in the novel *Wilhelm Meisters Wanderjahre* (Wilhelm Meister's Journeyman Years, 1821–29). This story, too, tells of love between an aging man, here a major, and a young woman, here his son's fiancée. Like Aschenbach, the major resorts to cosmetics to make himself look younger and more appealing. Finally, Mann's story bears traces of Goethe's *Faust* (1808–32). Mann once planned to emulate this famous tragedy, and *Death in Venice* has been thought to compete with it and to end, as it does, in apotheosis—that is, with the exaltation and deification of its hero.[8] Like the episode from his life that Mann often cited, Goethe's works thus may have left important marks on the novella.

A fourth modern author whose influence can be discerned in *Death in Venice* was French, not German: Gustave Flaubert (1821–90), the author of *Madame Bovary* (1857). In the first paragraph of the novella, Mann says that Aschenbach had not been able to halt the "motus animi continuus," the ceaseless motion of the mind, that the ancient Roman orator Cicero (106–43 B.C.E.) thought the essence of eloquence, of fluent and persuasive speech. Mann did not take this phrase from Cicero, however, who seems never to have used it, but rather from a letter that Flaubert wrote to his mistress, the poet and novelist Louise Colet (1810–76). That letter is dated 15 July 1853, and in it Flaubert attributes this phrase to Cicero. He also maintains that one should be as dedicated to art as the ancient Greeks, but write in modern, not classical, forms. One's writing should be powerful and strong and display a lust for life. These observations seem applicable to Aschenbach. He is dedicated to art, to be sure, but his style has become classical, and he is overwhelmed by the erotic energy and robust vitality that Flaubert praises here. He and Flaubert have the same first name, of course, a fact that hints at their similarity. His painfully slow and careful method of writing likewise recalls Flaubert, who was famous for his painstaking exactitude. Aschenbach thus seems to stand for the kind of modern novelist that, in real life, Flaubert represented. He is hardly as strong, however, as the authors or characters whom this renowned French namesake prefers in the letter that Mann indirectly quotes. Like the influences of Schiller, Platen, and Goethe, then, that of Flaubert seems complex.

Literary Influences: Ancient Greece

Death in Venice includes two allusions to Homer that are particularly revealing. In chapter 3, when Tadzio's sisters and their governess come down to breakfast, Aschenbach silently calls Tadzio—who is not with them, apparently because he is allowed to sleep late—"kleiner Phäake" (little Phaeacian). This is an allusion to book 8 of the *Odyssey*. The Phaeacians host the shipwrecked Odysseus, and their king tells him that they enjoy feasting, music, dancing, changes of clothes, hot baths, and beds. Tadzio is like this ancient people insofar as he, too, seems to like staying in bed. Aschenbach also cheerfully recites to himself a German translation of words spoken to Odysseus by that Phaecian king: "Oft veränderten Schmuck und warme Bäder und Ruhe" (Oft-changed jewelry and warm baths and rest) (8.249).[9] The fact that this line from the *Odyssey* occurs to Aschenbach as he thinks about Tadzio suggests not only that he is well read, but also that he muses about the boy in terms supplied by Greek antiquity and its art—here, by Homer's poetry. Mann alludes to the *Odyssey* again in chapter 4, when he tells how Aschenbach, relaxing on the beach at the Lido, remembers his summer home in the

Alps. It seems to Aschenbach that he is in Elysium, the otherworldly place where, in Greek mythology, the blessed live happily after death. As Mann describes it, this is a place "wo leichtestes Leben den Menschen beschert ist, wo nicht Schnee ist und Winter, noch Sturm und strömender Regen, sondern immer sanft kühlenden Anhauch Okeanos aufsteigen läßt" (where human beings are granted the easiest of lives, where there is no snow and winter, nor storms and pouring rain, but [where] Oceanus always lets arise a softly cooling breeze) (4.565–67). In Greek mythology, Oceanus was both a stream that ran around the earth and the god personifying this stream. Mann here renders in prose three lines of Homer's verse. In the *Odyssey*, those lines are spoken by Proteus, a shape-shifting god also known as the Old Man of the Sea. He foretells the death of Menelaus, the Spartan king whose wife, Helen, was abducted by the Trojan prince Paris in an act of elopement that started the Trojan War. It has been argued that Mann's use of these lines suggests that Aschenbach will die of the contentment that he feels in Venice.[10] One should note, though, that Proteus prophesies how Menelaus will go to the Elysian Fields, to the abode of heroes whom the gods have favored. Mann's second allusion to Homer, then, may suggest that Aschenbach, too, is such a hero and that he, like Menelaus, will be fortunate after death. Mann, not Aschenbach, makes this allusion. It therefore could imply that *Death in Venice* was meant to end by rewarding, not punishing, Aschenbach.

Mann also alludes to Xenophon (c. 430–c. 355 B.C.E.), the ancient Athenian historian. Xenophon was a student of Socrates, and his *Memorabilia* is his recollections of that famous philosopher. Aschenbach quotes two sentences from this Greek work in chapter 3. At the beach, he sees one of Tadzio's playmates, a Polish boy addressed as "Jaschu," kiss him. Aschenbach thinks that this second boy should flee the effects of that kiss. Quoting book 1, chapter 3, of *Memorabilia*, he thinks to himself, "Dir aber rat ich, Kritobulos . . . geh ein Jahr auf Reisen! Denn soviel brauchst du mindestens Zeit zur Genesung" (But I advise you, Critobulus, to travel for a year. For you need at least that much time to recover). In Xenophon, the original version of these sentences occurs in a passage showing how Socrates spoke and acted in ways that benefited his companions. He was pious, Xenophon notes, as well as temperate in matters of food, drink, and sex. One should refrain from having sex with people who are beautiful, he thought, for it is hard to be moderate with them. To reinforce this point, Socrates tells how he once saw Critobulus kiss the beautiful son of Alcibiades (c. 450–404 B.C.E.), the Athenian military leader and statesman. Socrates compares such kisses to the stings of poisonous spiders. He also observes that just looking at beautiful people, even without touching them, can drive one mad. He therefore tells Xenophon, to whom he relates this event, to flee if he sees someone beautiful. Furthermore, he tells Critobulus to go away for a year in order that the "sting" he has received from kissing the beautiful son of Alcibiades might heal. Like Mann's allusions to Homer, this one to Xenophon not only displays Aschenbach's erudition, but also hints at his psychological state. Aschenbach silently quotes these lines as if he were Socrates, speaking more wisely than he eventually acts. This allusion thus suggests how much Mann's hero will change by the end of the story.

Another Greek author to whom Mann alludes is Plutarch (46?–c. 120). Among the essays and dialogues collected in this ancient biographer's *Moralia* is his *Erotikos* (On Love). This work discusses the nature and basis of love, arguing that love is more than just carnal pleasure or sexual lust. *Death in Venice* includes several allusions to it. Three of them occur in chapter 4. As Aschenbach grows intoxicated from admiring Tadzio, Mann, reporting Aschenbach's thoughts, asks, "Stand nicht geschrieben, daß die Sonne unsere Aufmerksamkeit von den intellektuellen auf die sinnlichen Dinge wendet?" (Was it not written that the sun turns our attention from intellectual to sensual things?). Mann also observes that the soul is so delighted when the sun numbs and charms our memory and our reason that it clings to beautiful objects and can contemplate higher things only by means of a body. Just as mathematicians show children tangible images of pure forms, he writes, divine love makes the intellectual visible to us in the shape of human youth. He is referring to geometric figures here, and this analogy, along with his question and his thoughts about the sun and the soul, comes from Plutarch (765A). Aschenbach once again thus sees himself and his attraction to Tadzio in terms taken from ancient Greece. According to Plutarch, moreover, love may use the sight of beautiful youths to lead the soul away from mortal, sensible objects, toward divine, intellectual beauty and truth. In other words, seeing beautiful people can remind us of a higher realm where the human soul belongs. Will love perform this service for Aschenbach? He seems to be aware that it might, and at this point he sees in Tadzio beauty itself, the divine form or intellectual perfection that Plutarch discusses. A little later, Mann notes that Eros loves idleness. He is quoting a line from *Danae*, a play by the Greek tragedian Euripides (485?–406 B.C.E.). Plutarch, too, quotes this line (757A). Aschenbach soon tries but fails to talk to Tadzio, moreover, paraphrasing Plutarch (762F) when he thinks he is dismayed like a cock that lets its wings droop while it fights. Finally, in chapter 5, Mann—speaking, it seems, for Aschenbach—rhetorically asks if the bravest of nations did not respect homosexual love. Plutarch (761A) claims they did. Mann alludes to Plutarch, then, to show the effects of love, especially its power to restore human souls to their proper, intellectual sphere.

Mann's most important allusions to an ancient Greek author in his remarks on love, however, are to Plato (427?–347? B.C.E.). He adapts passages from two of Plato's dialogues: the *Symposium* and the *Phaedrus*. Like Plutarch's later *Erotikos*, both these dialogues state that love of human beauty can convey human souls to a realm of pure intellect. Unlike Plutarch's essay, though, which culminates in praise of conjugal love, the love of married couples, both dialogues are mainly about love between men. The *Symposium* comprises seven speeches in praise of Eros, the ancient Greek god of love. These speeches are given by guests at a dinner party in Athens. One of those guests is Socrates, whose speech is the highpoint of the dialogue. The philosopher reports how Diotima, a wise prophetess, taught him about love. Among other things, she described how a person properly initiated into the mystery of love rises on a ladder or a stairway that leads from the love of one beautiful body, to the love of all such bodies, to love of beautiful souls, to love of the beauty of customs such as laws, and finally to the love of the beauty of knowledge. In the end, such a lover sees the divine Form of Beauty itself. For Plato, reality ultimately lay in such abstract and unchanging ideal Forms. The love of beauty can thus lead to a love of wisdom and truth—in other words, to philosophy. In the *Phaedrus*, Socrates himself proposes an equally lofty theory of homosexual love. His argument is complex, involving issues such as the immortality, transmigration or reincarnation, and nature of human souls. The part that pertains most directly to *Death in Venice* is Socrates' palinode in praise of Eros, a recantation of an earlier speech. Here he maintains that love is divine madness and that it can be beneficial because it enables us to recollect the eternal Forms that our souls once saw in heaven, before they fell and entered bodies on earth. Love has this effect when a boy's beauty reminds his lover of Beauty, one Platonic Form, and when that lover resists the urge for sexual gratification. Not all lovers show such restraint. The few who do, however, lead a philosophical life. In its original sense, "Platonic love" is thus strong erotic energy channeled—speaking in psychoanalytic terms, one might say "sublimated"—into the highest of all possible pursuits. Without erotic attraction to human beauty, in fact, it might seem impossible, given Socrates' assumptions, to transcend or rise above the merely physical and recall abstract, ultimate truth or reality. This is clear in both the *Symposium* and the *Phaedrus*.

It is this elevating and ennobling kind of love, moreover, that Aschenbach has in mind when he watches Tadzio at the beach in chapter 4. Just after the passage that tells how the sun can turn our attention from intellectual to sensual things, Aschenbach envisions the setting of the *Phaedrus*. He imagines a plane tree not too far from the walls of Athens and a shady spot that smells of fragrant chaste-tree blossoms, where there are votive statues and offerings to the nymphs and the river god Achelous. He also "sees" a stream, chirping cicadas, and a grassy slope on which to rest one's head while lying. All these details are taken from Plato (230B–C). Two people are resting on this slope. One of them is young, beautiful, and lovable; the other is old, ugly, and wise. This is how Plato describes Phaedrus and Socrates. Aschenbach also imagines Socrates teaching Phaedrus about desire and virtue. As in the *Phaedrus*, Socrates speaks of a lover's startling images of eternal Beauty; of the desires of a base man, who cannot think of this Beauty when he sees such human images; and of the sacred fear that befalls a noble one when a godlike face or a perfect body appears to him. Mann, like Plato, says that such a noble man is beside himself, that he honors the boy who has such Beauty, and that he would sacrifice to the boy, as if the boy were the statue of a god, if he were not afraid that people would think him mad. As in the *Phaedrus*, moreover, Socrates notes that Beauty alone is both visible and lovable, the only form of the intellectual that we can know with our senses. Mann's Socrates sums up Plato's thoughts when he tells Phaedrus that beauty can be a means—but only a means—to intellect. He also makes two remarks that Plato's Socrates does not. First, Aschenbach imagines Socrates saying that we, like Semele, would perish and burn for love if reason, virtue, and truth—that is, other Platonic Forms—appeared to us. Semele was a mortal who died in this way when Zeus appeared to her. She was pregnant with a child by him then, with Dionysus, "the foreign god" so prominent in *Death in Venice*. Second, Mann's Socrates observes that a lover is more divine that his beloved. This idea comes from the *Symposium*, where Phaedrus, who gives one of its speeches, claims, "A lover is more godlike than his boy, you see, since he is inspired by a god."[11] Mann not only alludes to the setting and subject of the *Phaedrus*, then, but also makes a reference to Greek mythology and adds a line from the *Symposium*. He thereby uses Plato for his own narrative purposes, underscoring the dangerous sensuality—the carnal and sexual nature—of the perception of beauty. This sensuality is what bothers Aschenbach.

Mann's other allusions to Plato likewise serve larger narrative purposes in *Death in Venice*. Mann alludes to the *Phaedrus* again in chapter 5, when

Aschenbach, lost in the middle of Venice, muses about how riskily beauty mediates between the senses and the intellect. Exhausted and feverish, he once again hears Socrates telling Phaedrus that beauty alone is both divine and visible. He also hears Socrates saying that beauty is the path artists take to intellect, that artists therefore can never achieve wisdom or dignity, and that their reliance on their senses necessarily leads them astray. We poets, Socrates adds, are erotic, pathetic, and dissolute. Our style, our fame and honor, and the masses' trust in us are all laughable. Both knowledge and beauty lead us to the abyss. All these criticisms of artists and poets come from Mann, not Plato, and they constitute a crucial theme of Aschenbach's story. Mann's Socrates here voices Aschenbach's concerns, and Aschenbach hardly seems fit to instruct his Phaedrus, Tadzio, about metaphysical love. In contrast to Plato's Socrates, Aschenbach here seems drawn down by beauty, not up. This allusion to the *Phaedrus*, like the one in chapter 4, thus hints that Mann meant to tell how artists' sensuality destroys their dignity. Another possible allusion to Plato in chapter 5, however, seems at odds with this conclusion. It may occur in Mann's last scene, which is set at the beach. Aschenbach watches Tadzio linger "am Rande der Flut" (at the edge of the sea). After wading to a sandbar, the boy stands in front of the water, which is said to be nebulous, limitless, promising, and enormous. Mann is not quoting or paraphrasing Plato here, but his setting itself is reminiscent of a line in the *Symposium*. After explaining the ever-higher levels of the love of beauty, Diotima says there that a lover who has scaled them beholds "the great sea of beauty."[12] Mann's working notes contain an excerpt, in German translation, of the passage in which these words occur. He even underlined them. It thus seems legitimate to consider them a source of the setting of his final scene. If Aschenbach, looking at the Adriatic, is gazing at Plato's sea of beauty, moreover, he is a philosophical lover: he has risen, not fallen, in the end. Other allusions to both the *Symposium* and the *Phaedrus* are scattered throughout *Death in Venice*. The two or three cited here are the most important, though, since they are the most sustained and suggestive. Far more clearly than the others, they concern issues as well as interpretations that must be considered in any adequate reading of Mann's text.

Other Influences

Mann's knowledge of these ancient sources may not always have been direct. He read other, modern works that refer to them, and these works, too, influenced his story. One such work is *Psyche* (1890–94), a book about the Greeks' cult of the soul and belief in immortality. It is by the philologist—that is, the classical scholar—Erwin Rohde (1845–98), and Mann excerpted several passages from it in his working notes. He also made use of many words and ideas from these passages in his story. The lines from the *Odyssey* that he quotes in chapter 4, for example, the ones about the Elysian Fields, are also quoted in Rohde's chapter on *Entrückung* (transport). Their occurrence there is significant, for Mann says that Aschenbach feels "entrückt" (transported) to Elysium. When Mann adds that days there are "mühelos" (effortless), and when he later remarks that Eos, the goddess of dawn, rises from beside her husband Tithonos, he likewise uses words found in that chapter of Rohde's study. Mann's most important borrowings from Rohde, however, occur in Aschenbach's orgiastic dream in chapter 5. In that dream, Aschenbach hears noises and sees a landscape, animals, and frenzied worshipers that Mann describes in terms taken almost verbatim, almost word for word, from Rohde. Aschenbach fears, desires, and wants to know about these things, and he eventually overcomes his disgust and joins the enthralled celebrants of Dionysus. Rohde describes many of these same things in the initial chapter of the second part of his book. That chapter discusses the origins of the Greeks' belief in immortality. Rohde traces that belief to their cult of Dionysus and explains the ecstatic worship of this god as a "mania," a divine madness or religious enthusiasm. Mann, of course, has already told of Aschenbach's mania and enthusiasm, his exaggerated desire to follow the Polish family and his inspired interest in the elevating force of beauty. Here is how Rohde describes the worship of Dionysus:

> The festival was held on the mountain tops in the darkness of night amid the flickering and uncertain light of torches. The loud and troubled sound of music was heard; the clash of bronze cymbals; the dull thunderous roar of kettledrums; and through them all penetrated the "maddening unison" of the deep-toned flute, whose soul Phrygian *aulêtai* had first waked to life. Excited by this wild music, the chorus of worshipers dance with shrill crying and jubilation. We hear nothing about singing: the violence of the dance left no breath for regular songs. These dances were something very different from the measured movement of the dance-step in which Homer's Greeks advanced and turned about in the *Paian*. It was in frantic, whirling, headlong eddies and dance-circles that these inspired companies danced over the mountain slopes. They were

mostly women who whirled round in these circular dances till the point of exhaustion was reached; they were strangely dressed; they wore *bassarai*, long flowing garments, as it seems, stitched together out of fox-skins; over these were doeskins, and they even had horns fixed to their heads. Their hair was allowed to float in the wind; they carried snakes sacred to Sabazios in their hands and brandished daggers or else thyrsos-wands, the spear-points of which were concealed in ivy-leaves. In this fashion they raged wildly until every sense was wrought to the highest pitch of excitement, and in the "sacred frenzy" they fell upon the beast selected as their victim and tore their captured prey limb from limb. Then with their teeth they seized the bleeding flesh and devoured it raw.[13]

Rohde here uses four technical terms: "Phrygian *aulêtai*" are flute-players from Phrygia, a region in Asia Minor; "the *Paian*" is a hymn sung in thanks to the god Apollo or to the goddess Artemis; "Sabazios" is a name for Dionysus in Thrace, a region north of ancient Greece that Rohde thought was the home of Dionysus's cult; "thyrsos-wands" are staffs tipped with pine cones. Mann omitted all of these terms when he adapted this passage in *Death in Venice*. He also omitted Rohde's academic commentary, which would detract from the forcefulness of Aschenbach's impressions. He added much, too, most notably the *u*-sound that is the last vowel in "Tadziu," the vocative case of Tadzio's name. He mentions this sound twice, thereby reinforcing the fact that the Polish boy plays the role of the Greek god for Aschenbach. Elsewhere, Rohde calls Dionysus a god who is foreign to Greece, and in Aschenbach's dream he is called "der fremde Gott" (the foreign god). These omissions, additions, and equivalents show how Mann turned a learned and dry description into a gripping fictional scene.

Another work that influenced Mann was *Die Welt als Wille und Vorstellung* (The World as Will and Representation, 1819) by Arthur Schopenhauer (1788–1860). Mann read this book in 1899, and he quoted it in his first novel, *Buddenbrooks*. Chapter 44 of its second volume is entitled "Die Metaphysik der Geschlechtsliebe" (The Metaphysics of Sexual Love, 1844). In an appendix to this chapter, Schopenhauer cites several ancient Greek or Roman writings that mention pederasty, among them Plato's *Symposium*, Xenophon's *Memorabilia*, and Plutarch's *Erotikos*. In the chapter proper, he cites the *Phaedrus*, too. He thus refers to all the Greek authors besides Homer who have here been termed ancient influences. According to Aristotle, Schopenhauer also observes, people who are either too young or too old do not produce strong children. Nature prevents the birth of feeble ones, he maintains, by misdirecting men's sexual instinct. This accounts for the tendency to pederasty, he adds, that starts at about the age when a man, as Aristotle decrees, should not have any more children. That age is fifty-four. Mann's working notes suggest that Aschenbach is fifty-three, so he seems to have studied Schopenhauer carefully indeed. Both the title of Aschenbach's novel *Maja* and Mann's idea that the sea suggests nirvana also appear to have come from Schopenhauer. In Hindu philosophy, *maya* means "illusion," especially the unreality of the material world; in Buddhism, *nirvana* is a state of bliss attained by extinguishing one's own individual existence. These concepts play a major role in Schopenhauer's philosophy. Aschenbach thus seems to have written about the illusoriness of the world and to die, at the sea, in blessedness.

A third work that mentions at least one of Mann's Greek sources and influenced his story was Georg Lukács's *Die Seele und die Formen* (The Soul and the Forms, 1911). This critic and his remarks on the ethics of Prussianism in *Death in Venice* have already been noted above. In the essays that constitute this earlier work, he is concerned, as its title implies, with the problem of form. He treats this problem both in literature and in life, regarding the forms of literary texts as well as the relationship between form and the ways in which people, especially artists and intellectuals, live in modern, alienated society. In general, Lukács here address the same antagonism of life and art that Mann discusses in *Death in Venice*. In his essay on the French novelist Charles-Louis Philippe (1874–1909), moreover, Lukács comments on the idea of love that Socrates explains in Plato's *Symposium*. That essay is entitled *Sehnsucht und Form* (Longing and Form), and it contains a line that Mann quotes when he expands Plato's remarks on beauty in Aschenbach's second allusion to the *Phaedrus*. To Lukács, longing appears only as love: "In life, longing has to remain love: that is its happiness and its tragedy."[14] Aschenbach speaks some of these words, and others very like them, in German, when he exhaustedly sits in the middle of some Venetian square, having given up pursuing Tadzio. Half hallucinating, he hears Socrates address Phaedrus and say, ". . . unsere Sehnsucht muß Liebe bleiben—das ist unsere Lust und unsere Schande" (. . . our longing must remain love—that is our delight and our shame). Aschenbach is speaking of poets here, and therefore of himself. At the end of this scene, after other remarks on the debasing effect of poets' sensuality, he hears Socrates say, "wir vermögen nicht uns aufzuschwingen, wir vermögen nur auszuschweifen" (we cannot pull ourselves together, we can only fall apart). This is another reworking of a phrase taken from Lukács. In German, *aufschwingen*—here translated as "pull . . . together"—literally means "soar" or "take wing." Lukács uses a noun derived from this verb, *Aufschwung*, when he writes that people and poets do not transform their longing into philosophy and intellectual contemplation, as Socrates did: "But it will always be denied to men and poets to soar as high as this."[15] Lukács is not as pessimistic about love or beauty as Mann, who takes this idea to a new extreme. That Lukács both wrote words recurring in Mann's novella and later remarked on Aschenbach's Prussianism, however, shows how the historical, cultural, and sociological factors that figure in *Death in Venice* are related to the literary and other influences upon its author. Lukács gave one thing to Mann's story, that is, and got another out of it. This give-and-take suggests how that story contributed to its own international, intellectual context.

NOTES

1. For a fuller account of the foreign and domestic policies summarized here, see Dietrich Orlow, *A History of Modern Germany: 1871 to Present*, 3d ed. (Englewood Cliffs, NJ: Prentice-Hall, 1995), 62–94.

2. For fuller discussions of Frederick's character traits, see biographies such as Gerhard Ritter's *Frederick the Great*, trans. Peter Paret (Berkeley: University of California Press, 1968).

3. See Giles MacDonogh, *Frederick the Great* (London: Weidenfeld & Nicolson, 1999), 106, 195, 221–22.

4. Georg Lukács, *Essays on Thomas Mann*, trans. Stanley Mitchell (New York: Grosset & Dunlap, 1965), 119.

5. Ibid., 25.

6. Max Weber, *The Protestant Ethic and the Spirit of Capitalism*, trans. Talcott Parsons (New York: Scribner, 1958), 172.

7. Hans Rudolf Vaget, "Thomas Mann und die Neuklassik: 'Der Tod in Venedig' und Samuel Lublinskis Literaturauffassung," *Jahrbuch der deutschen Schillergesellschaft* 17 (1973): 432–54.

8. Werner Frizen, "Der 'Drei-Zeilen Plan' Thomas Manns: Zur Vorgeschichte von *Der Tod in Venedig*," *Thomas Mann Jahrbuch* 5 (1992): 125–41; and Frizen, "Fausts Tod in Venedig," in *Wagner—Nietzsche—Thomas Mann: Festschrift für Eckhard Heftrich*, ed. Heinz Gockel, Michael Neumann, and Ruprecht Wimmer (Frankfurt am Main: Klostermann, 1993), 228–53.

9. See Herbert Lehnert, "Note on Mann's *Der Tod in Venedig* and the Odyssey," *PMLA* 80.3 (June 1965): 306–7.

10. Franz H. Mautner, "Die griechischen Anklänge in Thomas Manns 'Tod in Venedig,'" *Monatshefte* 44.1 (January 1952): 20–26.

11. *Symposium*, 180B, trans. Alexander Nehamas and Paul Woodruff (Indianapolis: Hackett, 1989), 12.

12. *Symposium*, 210D, quoted in Nehamas and Woodruff, 58.

13. Erwin Rohde, *Psyche: The Cult of Souls and Belief in Immortality among the Greeks*, trans. W. B. Hillis (London: Kegan Paul, 1925), 257.

14. Georg Lukács, *Soul and Forms*, trans. Anna Bostock (Cambridge, MA: MIT Press, 1974), 94.

15. Ibid.

5 Ideas

Many ideas discussed in *Death in Venice* have already been noted in connection with its text or its context. Among them are writers' dignity, mastery, and status in a bourgeois world; ancient Greek notions of beauty, pederasty, and divinely inspired madness; and Prussianism, Protestantism, and literary modernism. Treating such ideas apart from an author's text, moreover, and thus out of context, is always risky. In any serious literary work, much depends not only on what is said, but also on who says it and on just how, why, where, and to whom it is said. Nonetheless, such ideas can often be considered in a more general way, as objects or products of thought that express and explain authors' wider interests and purposes. As noted above, for example, Mann made creative use of how the philologist Erwin Rohde had described the ancient Greek cult of Dionysus. The philosopher Friedrich Nietzsche, however, had defined the concept of the Dionysian in general, contrasting it with that of the Apollinian in a manner that can help make sense of Aschenbach's story. The Greek tragedian Euripides similarly presents Dionysus in a light that helps one understand Mann's hero. One can likewise appreciate how Mann deals with the idea of knowledge and with Aschenbach's "wiedergeborene Unbefangenheit" (reborn naiveté) by regarding his novella together with an essay by the German author Heinrich von Kleist. The ideas of aestheticism and decadence, moreover, figure both in that novella and in Nietzsche's critique of the composer Richard Wagner. Furthermore, Plato's *Symposium* and *Phaedrus*, dialogues discussed in the previous chapter as Greek influences on Mann, can help one comprehend the ideas of pederasty and homoeroticism. Finally, *Death in Venice* may be read according to Sigmund Freud's writings on sexual dreams and on discontent with civilization. Viewed in these general ways and in such broader terms, the major themes and issues of Mann's story may seem directly related to its current audience, to those who discover it now, nearly a century after he wrote it. In any case, knowing those issues and themes reveals that Aschenbach's fictional life is beset by several larger and perennial human problems.

DIONYSUS AND THE DIONYSIAN

The idea of the Dionysian plays a prominent role in *Die Geburt der Tragödie* (The Birth of Tragedy, 1872), a book by the philosopher Friedrich Nietzsche (1844–1900). As the full initial title of this book declares, Nietzsche links ancient drama to the spirit of music.[1] Its subsequent subtitle mentions Greeks and pessimism, that is, a gloomy view of good and evil in the world.[2] Nietzsche relates these several concepts—ancient tragedy, music, the Greeks, and pessimism—by positing two opposite tendencies in Greek art: the Apollinian and the Dionysian. Named for the gods Apollo and Dionysus, the two tendencies assume contrasting artistic and physiological forms. Sculpture and dreams are Apollinian, Nietzsche thinks, while music and intoxication are Dionysian. Apollo stands for mere appearances, he explains, for moderate restraint, and for the principle of individuation. This last term comes from Arthur Schopenhauer (1788–1860), another philosopher, and it connotes awareness of oneself as a particular person. Dionysus, by contrast, stands for reality, blissful ecstasy, and self-forgetfulness, that is, for reunion with other people and reconciliation with nature. Apollo represents beauty and illusions, in other words, while Dionysus reveals suffering and knowledge. Tragedy couples these two opposite tendencies. It presents an Apollinian image of Dionysus, the god who is embodied by its heroes. Tragedy also provides metaphysical solace by suggesting that life fundamentally goes on despite the destruction of such heroes. Tragedy thus helps make the horror and absurdity of human existence bearable. Nietzsche then tells how tragedy died. According to him, the playwright Euripides (485?–406 B.C.E.) did away with its Dionysian elements. The actual slayer of tragedy, however, he adds, was Socrates (469–399 B.C.E.). This famous philosopher was the first "theoretical man," and his emphasis on knowledge and on logic destroyed the musical and mystical essence of tragedy. Finally, Nietzsche foresees a rebirth of tragedy in the operas, or music dramas, of Richard

Wagner (1813–83). He quotes Schopenhauer's definition of music as the only art that directly represents the "will," the elemental life force. Music can therefore give birth to tragic myths, he reasons, which convey the Dionysian wisdom that we are part of that eternal and impersonal "will." Among many other things, Nietzsche also claims that "all that we now call culture, education, civilization, must some day appear before the un-erring judge Dionysus."[3] He thus sharply criticizes his own Socratic day and age.

It is odd that Nietzsche blames Euripides for eliminating the Dionysian elements of Greek tragedy. Nietzsche himself observes that Euripides con-cluded his career with a play that glorifies Dionysus. That tragic play is *The Bacchae*, and it can indeed be read as glorifying this god of intoxica-tion. It tells a gruesome tale. King Pentheus of Thebes, the capital of Boeotia, a region in ancient Greece, is the son of Agave. She has three sisters, one of whom is Semele, the mother, by Zeus, of Dionysus. Pentheus and Dionysus, then, are cousins. Semele has been killed by one of Zeus's thunderbolts, and Agave and her two other sisters have refused to believe Semele's story that this god fathered her child. The child, Dionysus, there-fore drives the three surviving and unbelieving sisters mad. They are roam-ing with other women on nearby Mount Kithairon, having become "maenads" or "bacchae," celebrants of Dionysus, who also goes by the name of Bacchus. Pentheus strongly disapproves of their behavior and of Dionysus's influence on them. Dionysus himself arrives in Thebes, dis-guised as a mortal, and Pentheus vainly tries to imprison him. Dionysus soon tricks Pentheus into dressing like a woman in order to observe the maenads on the mountain. Pentheus has taken a prurient interest in them, obsessed by the idea that they have run off to have sex. As a messenger later reports, they discover him hiding in a tree and literally tear him apart. Agave, still possessed by Dionysus, proudly brings Pentheus's severed head back to town. When she finally comes to her senses, she sees what she has done and understands that Dionysus has destroyed her family. No one in that family has shown him proper respect or reverence. Euripides may not have meant these awful events to glorify Dionysus but rather to condemn the irrational and inhuman consequences of worshiping him. Other readings of the play are possible as well.[4] In Nietzsche's opinion, though, *The Bacchae* renounced Euripides' Socratic leanings, albeit too late, for Dionysus was already chased off the tragic stage.

These ideas of Dionysus and the Dionysian pertain to *Death in Venice* on several levels. In its third chapter, for example, Mann tells how the white skin of Tadzio's face stands out like ivory against his dark golden locks. Mann thus seems to echo Euripides' lines about Dionysus's long blond curls and pale complexion. This parallel implies that Tadzio partly embodies Dionysus. The Polish boy, that is, seems to stand for the Greek god. Aschenbach's attraction to Tadzio would thus appear to be an attraction to all that Dionysus represents. If this conclusion is valid, what is one to make of Mann's novella? Does Mann allow Aschenbach to be punished and destroyed because he, like Pentheus, has failed to acknowledge Dionysus's divinity? *Death in Venice* is not about religion, but *The Bacchae* may be taken as a warning against suppressing irrational impulses, and this psychological reading makes sense when applied to Aschenbach. Or does Mann expose such impulses as inhumane, criticizing them because they can be cruel and degrading? Euripides seems to do this, and Mann may as well, once again on a psychological level. In any event, Pentheus lets it slip that he finds Dionysus good-looking, a fact that may make Aschenbach's admiration of Tadzio seem mythically tinged and deeply tragic. In Nietzsche's more abstract terms, one might also contend that Aschenbach begins as an Apollinian character, then becomes increasingly Dionysian. When he first sees Tadzio, for example, he thinks of classical Greek statues and dispassionately studies the boy's handsome features. Mann thus suggests the notions of sculpture, restraint, and beauty that Nietzsche associates with the Apollinian. Mann often notes the presence of music, moreover, not to mention Aschenbach's growing intoxication. These two attributes of the Dionysian are most obvious in his orgiastic dream, when he loses his sense of self and becomes one with the many celebrants. The god they hail, of course, is Dionysus. Does this mixture of Apollinian and Dionysian elements make *Death in Venice* tragic? Can Aschenbach be called a tragic hero? Does Mann offer metaphysical solace of the kind that Nietzsche thought tragedy did? Reading the novella in light of Nietzsche's comments raises these questions, and there may be more than one correct answer to them. Mann certainly does show Dionysus judging Aschenbach's culture, education, and civilization. In this respect, *Death in Venice* is indeed a very Nietzschean novella.

KNOWLEDGE AND "REBORN NAIVETÉ"

Nietzsche links both Socrates and Dionysus to knowledge, but he has two vastly different kinds of knowledge in mind. Socrates embodies logic, optimism, and scientific progress, he thinks, whereas Dionysus stands for the pessimistic but reassuring insight that the "will," the life force, persists in spite of individual suffering. Aschenbach gains both these kinds of knowledge, attaining a Dionysian wisdom only after he turns away from Socratic understanding. His drift toward the Dionysian is shown in the course of Mann's story and has just been noted above. Mann never shows his earlier rejection of Socratic knowledge. Chapter 2, however, tells how it happened. Mann there recalls how Aschenbach's story *Ein Elender* (An Outcast) demonstrated to an entire young generation "die Möglichkeit sittlicher Entschlossenheit jenseits der tiefsten Erkenntnis" (the possibility of moral resolve beyond the most profound knowledge). Aschenbach discovered this possibility himself. Early in his career, he worked knowledge too hard, achieving a high yield at the expense of future production. Mann does not say exactly what such agricultural terms imply, but he uses them when he discusses the younger Aschenbach's cynical attitude toward art and artists. Aschenbach's knowledge, then, has to do with his own artistic profession. It also concerns his notion of moral resolve. Knowledge, Mann adds, soon loses its bitter charm for noble and capable minds. *Ein Elender,* moreover, rejects what is objectionable and thereby turns away from moral skepticism, from sympathy with the abyss, and renounces the moral laxity of the principle that to understand is to forgive. This story thus attests to Aschenbach's "Wunder der wiedergeborenen Unbefangenheit" (miracle of reborn naiveté). But is moral resolve that goes beyond what one knows, Mann asks, beyond analytical and inhibiting knowledge, not an ethical simplification and thereby a force for what is evil, forbidden, and morally impossible? This passage is not terribly clear, but it is crucial to understanding *Death in Venice.* Aschenbach himself refers to it later, in the second of his visions that is modeled on Plato's *Phaedrus.* Writers reject analytical knowledge, he thinks Socrates says, because it has no dignity and strictness; it is understanding, forgiving, and without composure or form; it has sympathy with the abyss, indeed it *is* the abyss. Mann here repeats the idea that knowledge is some kind of unfathomable chaos. Again, he does not explain what he means. Before the events of *Death in Venice* begin, however, Aschenbach has clearly chosen to ignore both what he knows about his work and what might hinder his moral resolve. It also seems clear that Mann considers such willful ignorance morally risky.

On a personal level, Aschenbach's rejection of "Socratic" knowledge has serious consequences. Throughout the novella, Aschenbach avoids analyzing his own motives. He no longer knows his true feelings, it seems, or at least hesitates to admit them. As a result, those feelings, with all their complexity, overpower him. On a more theoretical level, the ideas of knowledge and of naiveté have already come up in conjunction with *Über naive und sentimentalische Dichtung* (On Naive and Sentimental Poetry, 1795–96), the treatise by Friedrich Schiller (1759–1805) to which Mann alludes in the opening paragraph of his second chapter and that is cited above as a literary influence. Positing two different kinds of poets, Schiller raises a seemingly insoluble question. How can a poet be "naive" after being "sentimental"? One might likewise ask how self-conscious writers can regain their artless spontaneity and intellectual innocence. Posed in a more general way, this question occurs in *Über das Marionettentheater* (On Marionette-Theater, 1810), an essay by the German author Heinrich von Kleist (1777–1811). Kleist asks and answers it, moreover, in ways that highlight Aschenbach's central dilemma. He does so in three stages. First, a ballet dancer named Herr C. tells why marionettes can be more graceful than human beings. Second, Kleist relates how a young man of sixteen saw himself in a mirror as he gracefully put his foot on a stool; thought of the *Spinario,* a statue of a boy taking a thorn out of his foot; and then could not repeat the movement without looking comical. Third, Herr C. mentions a bear that could parry any thrust made at it with a rapier and that was not fooled by feints. In each of these three examples, natural grace is opposed to consciousness. Kleist ties the loss of such grace, moreover, to Adam's and Eve's acquisition of the knowledge of good and evil. Recovering our innocence, he writes, would require eating of the Tree of Knowledge again. Herr C. makes this same point in scientific terms, saying that gracefulness can return only after knowledge has, so to speak, passed through infinity. Among other things, he also observes that we can reenter paradise, which is barred to us, only by some back door. Like Kleist, Mann is concerned with reversing a harmful effect of conscious reflection. That is what Aschenbach tries to do by renouncing knowledge. Both in Kleist's essay and in *Death in Venice,* moreover, this reversal seems to be an impossible ideal. At any rate, there is a concrete link between these two texts: when Aschenbach first sees Tadzio in chapter 3, he, too, is reminded of the *Spinario*.

AESTHETICISM AND DECADENCE

Two other ideas that prominently figure in Mann's novella are aestheticism and decadence. They are related, and defining them shows how they apply to his hero. The word *aestheticism* denotes an attitude or theory according to which aesthetic criteria are paramount—more important than moral, religious, educational, political, practical, or other considerations—in art and maybe even in life. In turn, the word *aesthetic* is used to denote attention and sensitivity to beauty and to art. *Aesthetics* is the branch of philosophy that explains beauty and art, and an *aesthete* is someone who appreciates or admires beauty and who cultivates, sometimes excessively, a refined artistic sensibility. All of these words are derived from ancient Greek ones that have to do with perception or physical sensation. The opposite of *aesthetic* would be *anaesthetic*, a word used to describe drugs that make one insensitive to pain. Aestheticism involves the contrary: heightened feeling and intense sensory perception. It thus involves what is sensual, that is, what affects or pleases the senses. Potentially, it can be sensual in a more specific way, for it can involve sexuality and desires of the flesh rather than, or more than, pleasures of the intellect. One's attraction to a painting or a statue that shows a human nude, for example, may not always be entirely spiritual. This ambiguity of what is sensual in the perception of beauty seems to be Aschenbach's problem. In any case, an emphasis on ideal beauty and form—an emphasis characteristic of aestheticism—was evident in the late nineteenth-century European literary and artistic movement known as decadence. Artists or writers associated with this movement were interested in sensual beauty and amoral aestheticism, in death and disease, and in feelings of weakness or consciousness of over-refinement. More generally, the word *decadence* describes a process, state, or period of decay or deterioration. Its Latin roots suggest a falling down or away, and one speaks in English of falling into decline. The English historian Edward Gibbon (1737–94) recounts, for example, the decline and fall of the Roman Empire. Such a decline is often linked to moral corruption. The word *decadence* also denotes physical enervation, or sensual indulgence, or widespread cultural stagnation. In its general as well as special, literary meanings, decadence, too, thus seems to be a problem for Mann's hero. At any rate, like aestheticism, it is a concept whose significance for understanding Aschenbach is clear from many events described and opinions expressed in *Death in Venice*.

When Aschenbach turns away from knowledge, he turns toward beauty, toward art. Accordingly, Mann often calls him an artist and notes his concern with artistic form. Mann also makes many general statements about art, artists, form, and beauty. So does Aschenbach himself. Both men find them morally questionable. Around the time when Aschenbach achieves "reborn naiveté," Mann writes, one observes an almost excessive intensification of his sense of beauty—a purity, simplicity, and proportionality of form that make his works seem masterful and classic. But is form, Mann asks, not two-faced? Is it not moral and amoral? It is moral insofar as it results from and expresses discipline, he explains, but amoral and even immoral insofar as it is morally indifferent and strives to subject morality to its rule. Mann is here referring to the concept of *l'art pour l'art*, of art for the sake of art, art made and appreciated purely for its beauty, apart from moral issues. Such questions have arisen, moreover, in the course of Aschenbach's career. The combination of his father's conscientiousness and his mother's impulses resulted in an artist, Mann writes, and in this particular artist. Aschenbach himself wants to grow old because he believes that only artistry fruitful at all stages of life can be called truly great, comprehensive, and honorable. Mann also notes that art has transformed Aschenbach's face and nerves. Art, he explains, is an elevated life. It engraves traces of imaginary and intellectual adventures in the face of whoever serves it, and it engenders nerves that are pampered, over-refined, fatigued, and curious. Art, that is, makes artists spoiled, overly elegant, tired, and inquisitive. On this same general level, Mann observes that the fame accorded works of art is due to sympathy, to some mutual understanding or agreement, between artists and their audience. When Aschenbach thinks that Tadzio's mother does not rear him as strictly as his sisters, Mann adds that almost all artistic natures innately respect injustice resulting in beauty. Aschenbach, too, makes general comments on art. Wondering what his stern ancestors would think of him, he recalls that he has led a life devoted to art and that art today is a war, an exhausting struggle in which one does not last long. Later, he believes that artists' sensuality keeps them from becoming truly wise and dignified and that education by means of art is a risky undertaking that ought to be forbidden. Both he and Mann thus stress the moral ambiguity of art and aestheticism.

This ambiguity is especially evident in Aschenbach's reactions to Tadzio. At first, his appreciation of the boy's form and beauty seems disinterested and dispassionate. In other words, it initially appears to be impartial and devoid of emotion. Later, though, it turns out to be extremely sensual and even sexual in nature. When Aschenbach looks at Tadzio for the very first time, he sees personal charm and the purest perfection of form. Neither in nature nor in art, he thinks, has he ever encountered anything this beautiful. At breakfast the next day, he admires him again, silently expressing his approval in the way that artists express delight with a masterpiece. The sight of the boy running out of the water and onto the beach makes him think about the origin of form, moreover, and Aschenbach, who creates beauty, is soon inclined in a fatherly way to Tadzio, who has it. When Aschenbach admires Tadzio lying on the beach, he also recognizes the will at work in the boy's statuesque body, since this same will is at work in him, too, when he liberates, from the marble mass of language, the slender form that he has envisioned, a form that he presents to people as the image of intellectual beauty. When Aschenbach sees Tadzio return to their hotel one evening, however, he regrets that words can only praise, not reproduce, sensual beauty. In all of these instances, such beauty seems the object of his purely aesthetic contemplation. This, at least, is how Aschenbach himself consciously thinks of it. When he writes a short treatise with Tadzio nearby, taking the boy's beauty as his stylistic model, though, and when he soon cannot bring himself to exchange a few sobering words with him, Mann makes two general comments on art and artists that make this treatise and its author's motive seem dubious. It is certainly good, he says, that the world knows only the beautiful work and not the conditions in which it arose, for knowing the sources of artists' inspiration would often confuse and shock the world and cancel the effect of art. Mann seems to suggest that those sources of artistic inspiration are sensual, even sexual. He also wonders who can decipher the essence and nature of artistry. Who can comprehend, he asks, its profound merging of discipline and dissoluteness? Art, he implies, requires as well as lacks moral restraint.

Besides thus linking Aschenbach and aestheticism, Mann ties him to decadence. He does so most notably in remarks on his hero's frailty and increasing fatigue. When Aschenbach leaves his apartment at the beginning of *Death in Venice* to take his fateful walk to the cemetery in Munich, he is agitated by the work he has done that morning, and he has been unable to take the nap he needs once a day, now that he is becoming ever more worn out. He has not left Munich, except to go to his summerhouse in the mountains, moreover, ever since his life has slowly begun to decline. At least ten years earlier, at the age of forty, he was already exhausted by the burdens and vicissitudes of his work. In fact, although he was always driven to achieve, his constitution had never been robust. His doctors prevented him from attending school, and he quickly learned that people like him did not lack talent but rather the physical basis that talent requires in order to flourish. He bore the tasks imposed on him by his talent, Mann says, on soft shoulders. Furthermore, Aschenbach has once written that everything great exists as a *Trotzdem* (Despite), that it exists despite hindrances that include physical weakness. When one regards the kind of fictional characters he likes to describe, Mann adds, one could doubt that there is a heroism other than that of weakness. This brand of heroism is appropriate to the times, Mann notes, and people like

Aschenbach, who labor on the brink of exhaustion, are the heroes of the age. Mann seems to be talking here about his own, actual day and age. The decadence implied by all his references to Aschenbach's infirmity and delicacy thus seems to have been, in Mann's opinion, an immediate and contemporary concern. In any event, the weather in Venice makes Aschenbach sick as he adversely reacts to a mixture of sea air and scirocco that both excites and enervates. This is not the first time that Venice proves detrimental to his health, not the first time that his body fails him there. Bad weather has forced him to leave the city once before, and he is upset and humiliated by this second physical defeat. He seems to know that his susceptibility to disease signals that his strength and his health are declining. This susceptibility, which his death appears to confirm, is a further mark of his decadence.

Aschenbach's decadence is not only physical; it is also mental and even moral. Like his health, his will is increasingly weak, and Mann's descriptions of it, too, show his decline and fall. The writing that stymies and agitates Aschenbach at the outset of the novella, for example, requires a supreme preciseness of will, an exactitude that he no longer seems to possess. He loves his work, indeed he almost loves the enervating daily battle between his growing fatigue and his tough, proud, and often-tested will. When he thinks of the passage that is now causing him trouble, however, and tries to overcome his writer's block, he abandons his attack with a shudder of unwillingness. The words *battle* and *attack* imply that Aschenbach resembles a soldier and that the act of writing is like a war. The excellence of his work, Mann accordingly adds, is due to an endurance of the will and to a toughness like those that once conquered his native province. Mann is here referring to Frederick the Great's conquest of Silesia in the 1740s. As noted above, in the discussion of historical factors that figure in Mann's story, Frederick was a king of Prussia. Aschenbach's will is thus a Prussian attribute and, as such, historically foreign to him. His reliance on it therefore seems unnatural. Perhaps that is why he speaks for those exhausted heroes of the age, for those whose achievements come from clever management of their resources and from an effort of their will. In any case, Aschenbach has difficulty enforcing his will, and it eventually yields to life on the Lido and succumbs to his Dionysian emotions. When he sees that the ominous gondolier is not taking him to the steamer station at Saint Mark's, as he has ordered, it seems to him that he must ensure that his will is done. When the gondolier refuses to turn back, Aschenbach sees no means of enforcing his will, and he gives up trying to do so, relaxing in his soft seat. The easy life at the beach later relaxes his will, and he is soon unable to will a sober recovery from the emotional intoxication Tadzio occasions. His will to resist his orgiastic dream is honest, moreover, but he soon tastes the indecency and the rave of going under. Mann uses the word *Untergang* here, a word that later occurs in the title of Oswald Spengler's *Der Untergang des Abendlandes* (The Decline of the West, 1918). This book treats the idea of cultural decadence. Mann mentions the impotence of Aschenbach's will so often, though, that his story may best be described in contrast to the title of Nietzsche's *Der Triumph des Willens* (The Triumph of the Will, 1906). Mann does not describe any triumph of the will, but rather its defeat.

Another book by Nietzsche helps explain how decadence informs Aschenbach's art. That book is *Der Fall Wagner* (The Case of Wagner, 1888). In *The Birth of Tragedy*, as noted above, Nietzsche praised Wagner for reviving the spirit of ancient tragedy in his operas. By the time he wrote *The Case of Wagner* sixteen years later, Nietzsche no longer thought that highly of the composer. In fact, his opinion of Wagner was extremely low. This is because Wagner and his music seemed decadent. According to Nietzsche, he is the artist of decadence, a typical decadent closely related to European decadence in its entirety, its protagonist as well as its biggest name. Nietzsche says that he himself is a decadent but that he comprehended and resisted decadence. Wagner, he claims, is one of the sicknesses from which he has recovered. Wagner, he adds, has also made music sick. Among the features of Wagner's style that Nietzsche dislikes is mere imitation of large forms for which he is not strong enough. Aschenbach's own large works are not the products of strength and endurance, but combinations of many individual efforts. His writing might thus seem similar to Wagner's music. Both, that is, might appear to possess a trait that Nietzsche considers characteristic of literary decadence, indeed of decadence in general: the whole is a calculated composite, an artificial artifact. At any rate, there are at least three suggestive parallels between Nietzsche's text and Mann's. Nietzsche says that Wagner's music persuades one's entrails, for example, and enchants the spinal cord. Mann uses some of these same words when he tells how the flutes Aschenbach hears in his Dionysian dream enchant his entrails. Nietzsche describes the enervating seductiveness of Wagner's opera *Parsifal* (1882), moreover, saying, "Never before has there been such a *deadly hatred* of the search for knowledge!"[5] Aschenbach's denial of knowledge has been noted above. Finally, when Nietzsche first tells how he reacts to Wagner's music, he explains how the composer's orchestral tone is harmful to him: "I call it *sirocco*. I break out into a disagreeable sweat. My good weather is gone."[6] Mann often cites such effects of the scirocco, the hot, humid wind that makes Aschenbach ill. Aschenbach reacts to Venice, that is, in the same adverse way that Nietzsche reacts to Wagner's music. These parallels re-inforce the ties that bind Aschenbach and Wagner throughout *Death in Venice*. Those stylistic, thematic, and biographical ties have been noted above. Aschenbach, it seems, is also affected by Wagner's musical deca-dence.

PEDERASTY AND HOMOEROTICISM

The sensual indulgence associated with the idea of decadence can in-clude sexual license. Homosexuality, in particular, has sometimes been regarded as an expression of moral decay or cultural decline. It has not always, however, met with such disapproval. The ancient Greeks, for ex-ample, sometimes took a different and far less dim view of it. As men-tioned above, in the discussion of literary and other influences on Mann's story, Plato's *Symposium* and *Phaedrus* both explain how one kind of ho-mosexual love can be elevating and ennobling. That kind of love is ped-erasty, the sexual love between a man and a boy. According to Plato's Socrates, pederastic relationships are most likely to be uplifting if they remain unconsummated, when they do not involve sexual intercourse. The two dialogues also reveal how such relationships were conducted and considered even when they were not Platonic, that is, when they did not transcend physical desire. This information is provided most completely— and most sympathetically—in one of the seven speeches that constitute the *Symposium*. In that speech, Pausanias argues that love is of two kinds. It can be either common, vulgar, and attached to the body, he contends, or heavenly, noble, and attached to the soul. The latter kind, he claims, is felt only for boys. Not all men attracted to boys are motivated by this higher kind of love, he adds, and there ought to be a law forbidding af-fairs with preadolescents. Furthermore, the customs regarding pederasty differ in the various parts of Greece. In some, Pausanias explains, it is indiscriminately approved; in others, it is always considered disgraceful. In Athens, such customs are more complex. There, it is more honorable to declare such love than to keep it secret, a lover is encouraged, and at-tempts at conquest are praised. Boys are guarded against their suitors, though, and mocked if they submit to them. A pederastic lover's behav-ior, then, is considered both noble and disgraceful. Pausanias thinks that this ambiguity reflects the Athenians' attempts to distinguish proper from vile love. The only honorable way to take a man as a lover, the only one that is neither servile nor shameful, he claims, is to do so for the sake of virtue. Both the man and the boy must approach the relationship appropriately, and "when the lover *is* able to help the young man become wiser and better, and the young man *is* eager to be taught and improved by his lover—then, and only then . . . is it ever honorable for a young man to accept a lover."[7] The emphasis on virtue also makes such relationships beneficial to the city as a whole. Socrates makes similar statements in the *Phaedrus*, most notably in the speech that he later recants in his palinode praising Eros. A lover, he explains, should improve a boy's mind and cultivate his soul; the rewards of such a lover's friendship are divine gifts. In certain places and under certain conditions in ancient Greece, then, pederasty could be pedagogical. Such homosexual eros, that is, could be educational.

Plato's qualified praise of this single kind of homosexual love helps understand Aschenbach's feelings for Tadzio. Mann's allusions to the *Symposium* and the *Phaedrus* are noted above in the discussion of his literary and other sources. So are the ways that he departs from these two dialogues to underscore the dangers posed to artists by their own, necessary sensuality. So is the possibility that Aschenbach rises in the end, rather than falling, to behold Diotima's "great sea of beauty." Being aware of Plato's remarks on pederasty, however, also helps determine to what extent and in what way *Death in Venice* is about homosexuality. That some of those remarks occur to Aschenbach as he looks at Tadzio or reflects on his strong attraction to the boy confirms that the issue of pederasty is crucial in Mann's story. Mann seems far more concerned with pederasty, moreover, than with homosexuality in general. The German word for *pederasty* is *Knabenliebe*, and Mann almost always uses the first part of it when describing Tadzio. He does so from Aschenbach's point of view, calling Tadzio a "Knabe." This word is used to denote a boy who is no older than about fifteen. Tadzio seems to Aschenbach about fourteen. Furthermore, like Plato's most philosophical lovers, Aschenbach and Tadzio never consummate their relationship. In fact, they barely have a relationship. Aschenbach never touches Tadzio. He never even speaks to him. They do exchange many glances, and Tadzio is aware of Aschenbach's interest in him, even though he may not fully comprehend it. Their relationship, such as it is, though, remains purely Platonic. When trying to make sense of Mann's story, one needs to bear both of these facts in mind, both that it describes a pederastic longing and that no one in it has sex. Otherwise, one's interpretation of that story might go to some unwarranted extremes. At one extreme, one might think Aschenbach's desire for Tadzio purely physical and dismiss his musing about form and beauty as so much camouflage or as so much self-deception meant to disguise or conceal his lust. To put it bluntly, one might think that *Death in Venice* tells of little more than a repressed homosexual lover, a dirty old man. At another extreme, one might find his desire purely spiritual and discount its sexual element as extraneous and incidental to other, less mundane matters. Mann's novella might then seem to be about anything but an older man's love for a boy. Some might think that Aschenbach leads a damnable life and meets a deserved end, dying for his sins. Others might say that he embraces his homosexuality, cruising parks in Munich and beaches in Venice as he gradually comes out of the closet. The truth seems to lie between these extremes. Aschenbach is not just an aging stalker, of course, nor is he utterly immune to sexual urges. One might come closer to that truth by distinguishing what is sexual from what is erotic. The two concepts are related, but the former, the sexual, can be taken to mean the act of gratifying erotic desires, while the latter, the erotic, can be taken to mean the act of arousing sexual excitement. If one draws this subtle distinction, one might say that, strictly speaking, *Death in Venice* is not about homosexuality, though it may be the greatest tale ever told about homoeroticism.

SEXUAL DREAMS AND CIVILIZED DISCONTENT

Medical attitudes toward homosexuality were changing at the time Mann wrote *Death in Venice*, a development due in part to theories proposed by Sigmund Freud (1856–1939). The novella may be read, in fact, according to ideas borrowed from two of Freud's writings. The first of those writings is *Über den Traum* (On Dreams, 1901). This book sums up his earlier remarks on the significance of dreaming and on the interpretation of dreams. It tells how a process called the "dream work" transforms latent, or hidden, thoughts into the manifest, or palpable, content of dreams. This process distorts such dream-thoughts by condensing, dramatizing, displacing, and revising them. They are repressed, Freud maintains, insofar as they are rejected by one's mental censorship and thus inadmissible to consciousness. Most dreams are disguised fulfillments of repressed wishes, moreover, and in adults such wishes are usually erotic. Every dream derives from a recent event or impression reminiscent of an earlier, significant psychical experience. The function of dreams is to guard sleep. Freud reports two of his own dreams that might seem to contain details significant to *Death in Venice*. First, he mentions seeing the Propyläen, a monumental entry gate that is a neoclassical portico, when he was once in Munich. It figures in a dream conveying doubts about his medical conscientiousness. The wanderer that Aschenbach sees at the cemetery in this same city, when his own professional efforts seem dubious, stands on such a colonnaded porch. Second, Freud reports a dream in which he linked Goethe's discovery of a sheep's skull on the Lido to the idea that age is no defense against folly. As noted earlier, Mann said that he initially meant his novella to be about Goethe, and Aschenbach is aging, and perhaps foolish, on this very same resort island near Venice. Be that as it may, some of Freud's concepts seem to recur in Mann's story. Aschenbach has several dreams, some of which seem to show such concepts at work. As he stands across from the mortuary chapel in Munich, for example, he envisions a tropical scene. Mann notes that he has just had an attack of wanderlust, a feeling he has long given up and unlearned. Mann also introduces this vision with the phrase "Seine Begierde ward sehend" (His desire became seeing). Aschenbach's puzzling and powerful daydream is thus an expression, it seems, of a repressed desire. He also goes into other dreamlike states. On the boat from Pola to Venice, he dozes off and hears the old dandy and ticket-taker speaking in confused dream-words. When he first sees Tadzio, his musings on art and form soon seem like the pleasant but empty whisperings of a dream. On the way back to his hotel from the train station, moreover, the sight of places from which he had just taken a painful leave is described as a comical, dreamlike adventure. The most telling dream in Mann's story, however, is the terrible one Aschenbach has after he learns the truth about the cholera epidemic. The Dionysian crowd in that dream howls the same *u*-sound that he has heard whenever Tadzio's playmates or relatives have called his name. They use its vocative form, the one used to address someone: "Tadziu! Tadziu!" Aschenbach's orgiastic dream thus seems to derive, as Freud says dreams do, from a recent occurrence. Mann reports Aschenbach's case of writer's block, moreover, using two words that also occur in Freud's writings: *Hemmung* (inhibition) and *Unlust* (unpleasure). Mann is not necessarily referring to psychoanalysis when he writes that Aschenbach's story *Ein Elender* conveys disgust with the indecent psychologism of the age. If he is alluding to Freud here, though, Aschenbach may not just have dreams that fulfill repressed erotic wishes; he may also reject the very idea of psychoanalysis.

A second of Freud's writings applicable to *Death in Venice* is *Das Unbehagen an der Kultur* (Civilization and Its Discontents, 1930). This study treats some of the same larger psychological and societal issues that are raised by Aschenbach's adventures. Above all, it tells how civilization restricts the demands of instinct. That instinct is both sexual and aggressive. Actually, Freud describes two separate instincts. The first is erotic, while the second is destructive. Both lead to his conclusion that civilization is largely the cause of our misery and that we would be happier without it. Instinctual impulses are frustrated in the individual, he explains, by cultural ideals that society imposes. Individual liberty and satisfaction are restricted, and instincts are renounced and often sublimated. This is especially true of Western European civilization, which severely impairs sexual life. An inclination to aggression is likewise sacrificed. This inclination is part of a death instinct, and Freud regards it as the greatest impediment to civilization, which it threatens with disintegration. Civilization is a process in the service of Eros, he explains, which unites humankind. Civilization evolves, that is, in a struggle between Eros and Death. Freud adds that aggressiveness can be internalized and directed against oneself as superego or conscience. It then causes a sense of guilt and a need for punishment by the external world. The loss of happiness due to a heightened sense of guilt, in fact, is the price we pay for our advance in civilization. These ideas shed new light on Mann's novella. Its hero's repressed desires, for example, may not be just a private matter, but also reflect the erotic compromises made by his society. Aschenbach's illness and death may also be punishment that he imposes, or that Mann metes out, for his forbidden wishes. His sublimated eroticism may cause him misery, moreover, but it still seems preferable to outward aggression, which blocks the progress of civilization as a whole. Freud, then, helps one see Aschenbach's psychological tensions in a broad social and historical context. Although an individual, Mann's hero, it seems, embodies a collective cultural malaise.

Freud's study of civilization and discontent also helps one understand Mann's story in more specific ways. Freud begins, for example, by discussing an "oceanic" feeling of something limitless and unbounded. In the last scene of *Death in Venice*, Tadzio stands in front of the nebulous limitlessness, as Mann somewhat vaguely puts it, as if he were pointing out and hovering ahead of Aschenbach into the promising and the enormous. Mann may thus hint at the early phase of ego-feeling or at a state of narcissism similar to the kind that Freud mentions in his remarks on this feeling. Some people, according to Freud, regard this feeling as the source of religious sentiment. Aschenbach is hardly pious, but he does worship Dionysus in his terrible dream, and his situation in the end is literally oceanic as he watches Tadzio wade out toward the mysterious sea. Freud also calls mania a pathological state in which a condition similar to that of intoxication by drugs arises. As noted earlier, Mann mentions mania when Aschenbach goes off in pursuit of Tadzio, and he often notes his increasing emotional intoxication. Freud says that the love of beauty that is characteristic of the aesthetic attitude, moreover, derives from sexual feeling and exemplifies an impulse inhibited in its aim. Mann's comments on the ambiguous sensuality of aestheticism are evaluated earlier in this chapter. With help from Freud, one might thus conclude not only that Aschenbach displays erotic as well as aggressive instincts, but also that he is narcissistic, pathological, and inhibited. Such connections and conclusions seem clearer in German than in English. For example, Aschenbach usually has no time to travel because he his too busy with the tasks set him by "sein Ich und die europäische Seele" (his self and the European soul). In German, the word *ich* generally means "I" or "self." In English translations of Freud, however, it is rendered as "ego." Likewise, *Seele* generally means "soul," but it is also the word that is translated as "psyche." Like *Hemmung* (inhibition) and *Unlust* (unpleasure), two other words used, as just noted, both by Mann and by Freud, *ich* and *Seele* in *Death in Venice* can thus be construed as specific, technical terms employed by psychoanalysis. The German word used in the title of *Civilization and Its Discontents* is not *Zivilisation*, by the way, but *Kultur*. Mann chose the latter word to describe the devastating effect of Aschenbach's terrible dream. Its events destroy "die Kultur seines Lebens" (the culture of his life). This phrase expresses a notion that seems similar not only to one that Freud discusses in this second book, moreover, but also to the one that Nietzsche entertained when he said, as noted above, that Dionysus will one day judge all that we call culture, education, and civilization. This double similarity in turn shows how closely the ideas that have been treated separately in this chapter are related in Mann's story itself.

NOTES

1. The full title is *Die Geburt der Tragödie aus dem Geiste der Musik* (The Birth of Tragedy Out of the Spirit of Music).

2. The subtitle of the second edition is *Oder Griechentum und Pessimismus* (Or Hellenism and Pessimism).

3. Friedrich Nietzsche, *The Birth of Tragedy* and *The Case of Wagner*, trans. Walter Kaufmann (New York: Vintage, 1967), 120.

4. See Paul Woodruff, Introduction to *The Bacchae*, by Euripides (Indianapolis: Hackett, 1998), xxix–xxxviii.

5. Nietzsche, 184.

6. Nietzsche, 157.

7. Plato, *Symposium*, trans. Alexander Nehamas and Paul Woodruff (Indianapolis: Hackett, 1989), 18 (184E).

6 Narrative Art

As noted at the outset of the previous chapter, the ideas conveyed by serious fiction are inseparable from their text and context. The *what* of such fiction, one might say, cannot be divorced from its words. Those words are chosen as well as arranged in a particular way, so one might also say that the *what* of fiction is inseparable from its *how*. This *how* is an author's narrative art. The noun or the adjective *narrative* derives from the verb *narrate*, which means to tell or relate, as when one tells a story or gives a description. A *narrative* is something narrated—for example, such a story or description of a fictional or an actual event. The word *narration* is likewise used to denote this sort of account as well as an act, technique, or process of narrating. A *narrator* is a fictional or an actual person who narrates. These definitions help one understand *Death in Venice*. They can help explain Mann's choice of verbs and nouns, his repetition of certain narrative elements, his symbols and images, and his sometimes ironic point of view. Some of his verbs are in past tenses; others are in the present tense. They accordingly have varying functions and differing implications. Some of his nouns are double-entendres, or have suggestive connotations, or are abstract compounds; others are constructed from adjectives. Mann repeats various sounds, words, sentences, actions, or episodes. Related to this doubling are the motifs of clothing and of posture; of falseness, isolation, and belatedness; and of foreignness. So are the techniques of foreshadowing later events and of raising, but then postponing the fulfillment of, readers' expectations. Mann's many symbols and images include a few expressly designated as such; some that seem clearer than others; hands, teeth, the weather, and the sea. The outer world of Venice is closely related to the inner world of his hero, moreover, and Mann neatly combines psychology and myth. Finally, one needs to know how much of Mann's story is told from Aschenbach's point of view and how Mann's opinion of Aschenbach may differ from that of his narrator. Drawing these distinctions requires understanding the concepts of free indirect discourse and of irony. Studying all of these narrative features proves that *Death in Venice* not only often mentions art, but also—with its select prose and seamless organization—itself *is* art.

VERBS AND NOUNS

Mann's verbs have varying functions and different implications, depending on their tense. Some are in past tenses. One of those past tenses is compound; the other is simple. The compound one is the past perfect or pluperfect tense. This tense is used to indicate or express an action that has been completed prior to some other past time or occurrence. It is called compound because it consists of two parts: the past tense of the auxiliary verb *to have* and the past participle of some main verb. For example, *had written* is in the past perfect or pluperfect tense in the sentence "I had written to her before she called." In this example, I wrote before she called. Both events occur in the past, but the first takes place further in the past than the second. Mann uses this tense several times in his first two paragraphs. He reports that Aschenbach *had undertaken* a walk, *had been* unable to stop the internal mechanism of his eloquence or to sleep, and *had sought* the open air. He also observes that a false high summer *had set in* as well as that the English Garden in Munich *had been* as sultry as in August and, in places, filled with coaches and pedestrians. Aschenbach *had surveyed* an outdoor café, moreover, and *had taken* the path home. Only now does Mann report an action in the other past tense, the simple one. This is the past tense, and it denotes or expresses an action or condition completed at a former time. It is simple because it consists of one part: the past tense of a given verb. As Mann writes, for example, a storm *threatened*, and Aschenbach *waited* for the streetcar. Mann has already used this tense in his first two paragraphs, but only to describe conditions, not actions. He tells readers what Aschenbach's name *was*; that the year "19..." *displayed* a threatening mien, a phrase suggesting the political setting of his story; that Aschenbach's daily nap *was* necessary; and that it *was* the beginning of May. Not until Mann writes that the storm threatened and Aschenbach waited do the events of *Death in Venice*, strictly speaking, start. This distinction matters because it is not only temporal but also logical. The events that occur as Aschenbach waits for that streetcar—his sighting of the wanderer and his vision of a tropical landscape—occur not only after he grows agitated and tired but also because he feels this way. His agitation and fatigue, then, not only precede this sighting and vision, but also precipitate them. The same alternation between the pluperfect and past tenses occurs in Mann's second chapter, the one that tells about Aschenbach's career prior to the events of the novella proper. Here, too, temporal priority is logical priority. That career causes these events, which would not happen, or at least not in the way they do, if his life had not been as strenuous, strict, and devoted to his work. Mann's verbs in the simple past tense tell what occurs or obtains in the present time of his story, that is, while his verbs in the pluperfect tense suggest why what he describes has come to pass or to be the case.

Mann also uses some verbs in the present tense. He does so in three ways. First, he uses the present tense to make a chain of events seem more immediate. Such chains can be either brief or extended. Two brief ones occur in his third chapter. Aschenbach, having been rowed to the Lido, goes to a nearby hotel for change to pay the gondolier. Mann switches from the past to the present tense in this short episode. Aschenbach, he reports, *left* the gondola and, since he *lacked* change, *went* to the hotel. He *is* served, as Mann writes in the present tense of the passive voice, he *turns* back, and he then *finds* his luggage in a cart on the quay. Mann similarly changes from the past to the present tense when Aschenbach leaves his hotel for the steamer that will take him to the train station. He *made* to depart, Mann notes, *gave* tips, *was* sent off by the manager, and *left* the hotel. He *reaches* the steamer landing, though, and *takes* a seat. Both these examples suggest a rapid series of events, and both occur at turning points in Mann's story. The third chapter also contains two longer such series. Still aboard the boat that has taken him to Venice, Aschenbach orders a gondola. Someone *approves* his plan and *calls* his request down to the gondoliers, who *argue* with each other. His trunk *is being* pulled and dragged down the gangplank; thus he *is* prevented from disembarking. He *sees* himself incapable of escaping the old fop, whom drunkenness *emboldens*. This dandy *bleats* farewell, he *drools*, he *closes* his eyes, and he *licks* the corners of his mouth. His goatee *bristles*, he *stammers*, and his dentures *fall* onto his lower lip. Like the scene in which the gondolier disappears, this one in which the fop takes his leave is pivotal—and in the present tense. Another such scene takes place when Aschenbach arrives at the train station. His vaporetto *approaches* the station, his pain and perplexity *increase*, departing and returning both *strike* him as impossible. He *enters* the station, it *is* very late, and he *has* not one moment to lose. He *does* and *does* not want to make his train. Time *presses* and *flogs* him forward. He *hurries* to buy a ticket and *looks* around for an employee from his hotel. This fellow *shows* himself and *announces* that Aschenbach's trunk has been sent to Como. It *comes* to light that the trunk was misdirected back on the Lido. A last such example of this use of the present tense occurs in Mann's fourth chapter, when Aschenbach almost speaks to Tadzio. He *reaches* him, *wants* to lay his hand on Tadzio's head or shoulder, and a word, a friendly phrase *is* on the tip of his tongue. He *feels* that his heart *beats* like a hammer, he *hesitates*, and he *tries* to control himself. He *fears* that he has been following the boy too long, *fears* that Tadzio might notice him, *makes* a final attempt, *fails*, *renounces*, and *walks* on by. The present tense makes this scene, too, seem more immediate and less removed from Mann's reader.

Mann's second way of using the present instead of a past tense is to state a fact that is true, or at least seems to have been so, at the time when his story is told and at other times as well—true in the actual world, that is, not just in his fictional one. His statements of this kind refer to architecture, topography, and meteorology. They also refer to music, to the age in which he wrote, and to the beauty that he had perceived. When he mentions the stonemasons' shops near the cemetery in Munich, he says that their crosses, headstones, and monuments *constitute* a second, uninhabited cemetery. Such shops still exist there today. He adds that the mortuary chapel across the street *displays* gilded liturgical sayings about life after death. This chapel and these sayings, too, still exist, though the particular sayings that Mann cites are nowhere to be found. Similarly, Mann writes that two apocalyptic animals *guard* the stairway leading up to the chapel. No such animals can be found there now. If they were not there in Mann's day either, then they, like the two liturgical sayings he quotes, may be details that he invented to make this scene seem more ominous and more predictive of an unhappy ending. For that matter, the chapel is at street level, at least today, so the wanderer's elevated and elevating standpoint, too, may be a detail that Mann added for greater effect. He thus may have embellished the actual facts about the chapel with fictional additions. Most of his other facts stated in the present tense are less complicated. He mentions the avenue that *runs* across the Lido to the beach. This street is visible on a map of the island. He also notes the disgusting state that the sea air and scirocco *can* produce and that *is* at once exciting and enervating. Mann writes as if this state were well known. He also observes that the city of Venice inspired musical tones that *rock* and *lull* one to sleep. This sentence seems to allude to Richard Wagner (1813–83), the composer who, as was noted earlier, wrote part of his opera *Tristan und Isolde* (1865) while living in Venice. Mann appears to think that all listeners find Wagner's music soporific. In his second chapter, Mann also writes that Aschenbach spoke for all who *labor* on the brink of exhaustion and at least temporarily *attain* the effects of greatness. There *are* many such moralists of achievement, he says, and they *are* the heroes of the age. As explained earlier, Mann seems to be talking about his own day and age here. Finally, in his fourth chapter, Mann writes that Tadzio *is* too beautiful for words. He does this in a passage narrated from Aschenbach's perspective, but the present-tense *is* seems to indicate that Mann himself felt unable to express the boy's beauty, or at least that of his real-life model. Most of his story is told in past tenses, so this present-tense verb, like his others, stands out and interrupts the normal flow of his narrative.

Mann's third way of using the present tense is to offer psychological insights that make Aschenbach's experiences, including his passion, seem typical of human nature at large. In chapter 2, many of Mann's statements about art, literature, and knowledge are in the present tense. So is his pronouncement that only eternal bohemians *find* it boring and *are* inclined to mock when a great talent *outgrows* its adolescent excesses, *accustoms* itself to asserting intellectual dignity, and *assumes* the stern manners of its painful and powerful solitude. This sentence appears to justify Aschenbach's artistic development. In chapter 3, Mann notes that a solitary person's observations and encounters *are* both more blurred and more penetrating than those of someone sociable, his thoughts both more ponderous and strange and tinged with sadness. Such a solitary person's images and perceptions *occupy* him unduly, *deepen* in silence, and *become* meaningful. Solitude *occasions* what is original, beautiful, and poetic. Solitude also *occasions* what is perverse, disproportionate, absurd, and forbidden. This insight explains why Aschenbach is still bothered by thoughts of the fop and the gondolier even after he is settled in his hotel. It also seems to anticipate the ambiguous feelings he will later have for Tadzio. In any case, Mann also observes that to rest at perfection *is* the yearning of whoever *troubles* himself with the excellent. And *is* nothingness, he asks, not a form of perfection? This passage explains the profound reasons for Aschenbach's love of the sea. It is possible, moreover, that these thoughts occur to Aschenbach himself, whom Mann describes as emptily dreaming. When Aschenbach soon sees Tadzio express scorn for the Russian family, Mann adds that the serious observer of passion *resists* making use of what he perceives. Aschenbach's delicacy, though, does not prevent him from considering the boy worthy of closer attention now. In chapter 4, Mann's remarks about the dubious origins of art and the ambiguous nature of artists are in the present tense. He also says that an author's good fortune *is* a thought that *can* completely become feeling, a feeling that *can* completely become thought. This dictum is a transition between Aschenbach's image of Plato's *Phaedrus* and his attempt to write by taking Tadzio's proportions as his model. It thus seems to legitimate the erotically inspired writing that Mann questions a few lines later. Before describing how Aschenbach's and Tadzio's eyes sometimes meet, Mann adds that nothing *is* stranger or more ticklish than a relationship between people who *know* each other only with their eyes, who *encounter* and *observe* each other daily or even hourly yet *are* required to appear indifferently unacquainted. Between such people there *is* restlessness, curiosity, hysteria, and tense respect. One human *loves* and *respects* another, Mann observes, as long as he *cannot* judge him, and yearning *is* the product of insufficient knowledge. While this statement helps account for Aschenbach's interest in Tadzio, it also hints that his interest results from ignorance. Similar remarks on passion can be found in chapter 5. Aschenbach takes satisfaction in knowing that the Venetian authorities are covering up the cholera epidemic. This, Mann writes, is because passion, like crime, *is* not compatible with everyday order. Every confusion and affliction *must* be welcome to it, for it *can* hope to take advantage of them. Aschenbach is keen to hear the vulgar sounds of the street singers, moreover, because passion *paralyzes* discerning taste and seriously *entertains* charms that sober reflection *would* take lightly or dismiss. Finally, when Aschenbach is not inclined to warn Tadzio's mother about the epidemic, Mann writes that people who *are* beside themselves *abhor* nothing more than reflection. These final remarks sound sympathetic as well as critical, explaining without excusing.

Like his verbs, Mann's nouns have differing forms, functions, and implications. Some lend the events of his story further significance with their double meanings and revealing connotations. Others are compounds that convey a high level of abstraction. In these respects, they resemble other parts of speech and turns of phrase he employs. The old man at the landing on the Lido, for example, quips that Aschenbach has come for nothing. Like the German word *umsonst,* the adverbial phrase "for nothing" not only means that Aschenbach has not had to pay his vanished gondolier; it also hints that he has traveled to Venice in vain, that he will not find what he seeks there. To the extent that he has come for a rest, this suggestion proves accurate. When Aschenbach comes back to his hotel after failing to catch his train, the elevator operator says, in French, "Pas de chance, monsieur." This phrase, too, has two meanings. It suggests that Aschenbach had bad luck at the station as well as that he has no chance—that there is no way—of his getting what he wants, now that he has returned. When Mann tells how Aschenbach watches the sun rise and how the rest of the day is elevated and mythically transformed, he notes that his hero dwells in a divinely distorted world full of panic life. The adjective *panic* indicates that Aschenbach is under the spell of Pan, an ancient Greek fertility god known for his amorous adventures. Since Pan suddenly came upon people in isolated spots, *panic* also suggests terror and fear, especially if they are infectious or contagious. This single word thus links mythology, sexuality, and disease—as *Death in Venice* does as a whole. Furthermore, the hotel barber, head of the street singers, and English clerk all refer to cholera as "ein Übel." In German, this noun means both "illness" and "evil." It makes the epidemic seem unethical and hints that the medical issue is a moral one. Mann also uses compound nouns, most notably in his final scene. Tadzio walks "vorm Nebelhaft-Grenzenlosen." In the plot summary given earlier, this phrase is translated as "in front of the nebulous limitlessness." The literal translation is "before the nebulous-limitless." Mann constructs another such compound when he writes that it seems to Aschenbach as if Tadzio were pointing out and hovering ahead "ins Verheißungsvoll-Ungeheure." In the plot summary, the English equivalent of these words is "into the promising and the enormous." A more literal rendering is "into the promising-enormous." In both of these instances, Mann invents a compound noun by joining two adjectives. Both these nouns, moreover, imply a realm that lies beyond this world and beyond the power of existing words to describe. Both are also extremely abstract, and Aschenbach's inkling of this place could be visionary, perhaps even mystical. Like Mann's double-entendres and words with revealing connotations, these nouns suggest narrative dimensions far larger, then, than the naturalistic one in which the external events of his story occur.

These compounds are not the only nouns that Mann constructs from adjectives. He also turns adjectives into nouns in another way, most often when describing either Aschenbach or Tadzio. This way is more common in German than it is in English. One says in English, for example, that there is no rest for the wicked. The adjective *wicked* here stands for "wicked people." The noun *people* is not stated, but it is implied. The adjective itself thus serves as a noun. One does the same thing, and more frequently, in German. In fact, one does it with participles as well. A participle is a verbal adjective. It can qualify a noun, just as regular adjectives do. A present participle ends in *-ing*, while a past participle takes endings such as *-d, -ed, -n, -en,* or *-t.* One speaks in English of "the accused," for example, and means "the accused person." Theoretically, one might speak of "the accusing" as well and mean "the accusing person." This second participial noun sounds strange in English, but nouns like it often occur in German. Mann uses all these kinds of adjectival nouns when he describes Aschenbach, especially in chapter 5. They follow forms of *der* (the), the definite article for masculine nouns in German. This article differs according to the case of each noun. The adjectival constructions referring to Aschenbach in chapter 5 are: "der Reisende" (the traveling), "dem Abenteuernden" (the adventuring), "der Verwirrte" (the confused), "des Betörten Denkweise" (the infatuated's manner of thinking), "der Einsame" (the solitary), "der Verliebte" (the in love), "der Starrsinnige" (the stubborn), "der Berückte" (the enchanted), and "dem unter der Schminke Fiebernden" (the under the makeup fevering). All of these adjectival nouns shift the emphasis away from Aschenbach and toward his attributes. At this point, it seems, Mann says less about a particular person than about traveling and adventuring and being confused, infatuated, solitary, in love, stubborn, enchanted, and fevering. These qualities, in other words, appear to be more important than the individual who possesses them. Indeed, the lack of actual nouns in these constructions suggests that Mann's story has become impersonal and detached. At any rate, this lack suggests that his principal character is not as important as these characteristics. An emphasis on such general traits rather than on a specific person is similarly evident when Mann uses adjectival nouns to describe Tadzio. Constructions referring to him include "den Ruhenden" (the resting), "dem Begehrten" (the desired), and "des draußen Schreitenden" (the out-there striding). The adjective most often used to describe him, however, is *schön* (beautiful). It occurs over and over in nouns that denote him. What Aschenbach sees in the pretty boy, it seems, is the beautiful. This is especially evident in chapter 5, where such nouns made from *schön* and referring to Tadzio occur most regularly. Like Aschenbach, Tadzio thus seems less individual and more abstract toward the end of Mann's story. Aschenbach also sees, or thinks he sees, in Tadzio "das Bewunderungswürdige" (the worthy of admiration) and, just before he first recalls Plato's *Phaedrus,* "das Schöne selbst" (the beautiful itself). These two nouns are neuter, not masculine, a grammatical fact indicated by their article, *das*. They are not directly linked to any human male and are therefore even more abstract than Mann's other, masculine adjectival nouns. Since these nouns are often awkward in English, this level of abstraction and impersonality so crucial to *Death in Venice* is often lost in translation.

REPETITION

Another aspect of Mann's narrative art is repetition. He repeats various elements of his story. The smallest such elements are individual sounds, words, or sentences. The *u*-sound at the end of Tadzio's name in the vocative case—in "Tadziu"—is described in two places. Aschenbach initially hears it when friends or female family members call to Tadzio at the beach, then again from the revelers in his orgiastic dream. Mann mentions this sound twice both times, stressing its significance and the aural connection between Tadzio and Dionysus. He also repeats the word *Physiognomie* (physiognomy). The ticket seller on the boat, Mann says, has the physiognomy—that is, the facial features—of an old-fashioned circus director. The gondolier's physiognomy, he adds a few pages later, is unpleasing and even brutal. Repeating this word underscores a subtle link between these men, both of whom are uncanny and convey Aschenbach to his final destination. In one such repetition, the word that Mann uses is slightly varied. When Aschenbach sees the dandy on the boat, and then is confronted by him, Mann notes twice that the world seems strangely distorted. He uses the related words *Entstellung* (distortion) and *entstellen* (distort). He thus seems to stress that Aschenbach's impression of the fop may not be entirely accurate, a possibility that he raises when he first uses one of these words. In another repetition, Mann actually puts an earlier passage in quotation marks. When Aschenbach sees Tadzio's teeth in the elevator, he thinks that the boy is sickly and probably will not grow old. He thinks this thought again, and in the same words, when he sees Tadzio standing nearby at the street singers' performance. Mann may be hinting here that beauty is always fragile or even that Aschenbach would like Tadzio to die young so that he never loses his youthful, extremely good looks. When the merchant and the street singer answer Aschenbach's questions about the epidemic in identical terms, saying that the scirocco is oppressive and unhealthy, repetition is a way to highlight their collusion. Aschenbach reads about the epidemic in the German newspapers at his hotel, moreover, and one of his thoughts in this scene is "Man soll schweigen" (One should keep silent). This sentence recurs when he has decided not to warn Tadzio's mother to leave Venice. That it occurs twice stresses his complicity with the corrupt Venetian officials whose denials of an epidemic are reported in the papers. In the later scene, he even whispers this sentence aloud. He also whispers, "Ich werde schweigen" (I shall keep silent). In the earlier one, there is similarly a related sentence, "Man soll das verschweigen" (One should hush it up). The repetition and variation of this sentence leave no doubt that he expressly decides not to say anything and that he makes a public issue his own private matter. None of these repetitions, then, is merely mechanical. Instead, all of them lend *Death in Venice* further possible meaning.

Mann also repeats some of the actions or episodes he describes. They, too, often involve a repetition of certain words, and they, too, occur more than once for a reason. While Aschenbach's ship is awaiting medical inspection, it is repulsive to see the fop's drunken state. Among other things, he licks the corners of his mouth in a disgustingly ambiguous way. This suggestive gesture recurs when the lead street singer uses facial expressions and physical movements, including lolling his tongue in the corner of his mouth, to accompany a song in a manner that makes it ambiguous. The repetition not only connects these two odd characters but also hints at the ambiguity of their actions. Both men and the gesture that both of them make, Mann implies, seem mildly obscene. Similarly, Aschenbach eats strawberries twice. The first time, he is at the beach, having just seen the boy called "Jaschu" kiss Tadzio. He has also just recalled the passage from Xenophon's *Memorabilia* in which Socrates says that one should refrain from having sex with people who are beautiful. In Mann's scene, the strawberries are large and ripe, and it is very warm. The second time, Aschenbach has just lost sight of Tadzio in the streets of Venice. Now, too, he buys and eats strawberries, although they are overripe and soft. The English clerk has already told him that the food supply is probably infected. It thus seems that Aschenbach consciously ignores the imminent danger of contracting cholera. Given the erotic passage he quotes when he first eats them, the repetition may also hint that he is prepared to run the risk posed by sexual intemperance and immoderation. In any event, he soon finds himself back in the same remote square where, weeks ago, he vainly decided to leave Venice. Then, he sat there on the edge of a fountain. He does so again now, feeling even sweatier and more feverish than before. Now, too, he recalls an ancient Greek author's comments on beauty, the ones from Plato's *Phaedrus* about how only beauty is at once visible and divine. He also imagines Socrates adding that artists, whose path to the intellectual leads through the senses, can never achieve wisdom and dignity. By returning Aschenbach to this location, Mann reminds readers of how close his hero came to escaping a threat that has increased, a fate that seems inevitable. The English clerk, moreover, reports that the cholera epidemic comes from the delta of the Ganges River in India, a primeval, island wilderness in whose thickets tigers crouch. He thereby recalls Mann's description of the tropical landscape that Aschenbach envisions in Munich. It, too, is primeval and contains islands, morasses, and a crouching tiger. In retrospect, thanks to these repeated details, Aschenbach's vision seems to have been a premonition. Aschenbach himself remembers both the mortuary chapel and the wanderer before he decides to be silent about the epidemic. Now, he cannot bear the idea of going back to where he saw them, which shows how far removed he has grown from his old work ethic. Mann also repeats an episode that occurs before his story begins. The thick, humid air in Venice has made Aschenbach ill on some prior occasion. Mann says nothing more about this prior trip, but Aschenbach's sickness, too, is worse the second time around.

Besides doubling such sounds, words, sentences, actions, and episodes, Mann repeats narrative elements that function as motifs. A motif is some recurring element, theme, or idea that is distinctive and developed in a work of art. Motifs occur in music as well as in literature. As noted above, in the chapter about the text of *Death in Venice*, Mann admired the musical themes known as "leitmotifs" in Wagner's operas. As is also noted there, he uses such motifs in his novella. The example given above is the similar physical features possessed and similar articles of clothing worn by the wanderer, the gondolier, and the street singer. Those features and articles connect these sinister men, underscoring their role as links in a single, logical chain that binds the beginning, the middle, and the end of Mann's story. Other items of clothing, especially red ones, have further, related functions. When Mann introduces the manager at Aschenbach's hotel, he describes him as small, quiet, and polite, with a black mustache and a French frock coat. The next time that this character appears, he is said to be small, quiet, and in his French frock coat. The time after that, he is small, mustachioed, and in his frock coat. When Aschenbach later questions him about the epidemic, he is likewise small, quiet, and in his French frock coat. Thanks to such repeated descriptions of his manners and coat, readers should remember how this hotel manager acts and looks. Repetition is a way to remind readers and give them a clear impression of this character. Mann also mentions Tadzio's clothing several times. When Aschenbach first sees him, the boy is wearing an English sailor suit.

Tadzio comes to breakfast the next morning wearing a different suit, one that has blue and white stripes and, on its breast, a red satin ribbon. Later, at the beach, Aschenbach easily sees him because this red ribbon is so obvious. Later still, from the window of his room, he again sees Tadzio in the striped suit with the red ribbon. In chapter 4, the boy is in a blue-and-white bathing suit; in chapter 5, he watches the street singers' performance in a belted white suit; and in the last scene, he again wears his striped suit with the red ribbon. These repeated descriptions not only give Mann's readers a good idea of Tadzio's wardrobe, thereby reinforcing a consistent image of him; they also link the boy to other characters. The connection is the color red, which is also worn by the old dandy and later by Aschenbach himself. On the boat, the dandy wears a red tie, and the makeup on his cheeks is crimson. The makeup that the barber applies to Aschenbach's face is similarly carmine, and the tie that Aschenbach now wears, like the dandy's, is red. The color red, then, shows both how Aschenbach eventually comes to resemble a character he once found disgusting and that Tadzio is connected to the two of them. This same color ties Tadzio to the wanderer, gondolier, and street singer, who all, as noted earlier, have red or reddish eyelashes or eyebrows.

Another motif that links and characterizes these figures is posture. Two of them stand, and one sits. The wanderer and Tadzio, for example, stand in a similar way. The wanderer props his left arm on his side and crosses his feet. When Tadzio listens to the street singers, he props his left arm on a balustrade and his right hand on his hip as he, likewise, stands with his feet crossed. When he turns to face the beach in the final scene, he again has his hand on his hip. These similar descriptions imply that these characters are alike. Indeed, they not only strike similar poses; in the last scene, like the wanderer in the first, Tadzio appears to summon Aschenbach to some distant realm, some other, faraway world. In this scene, Mann also calls the boy a pale and a lovely "Psychagog" (psychagogue). This word means "conductor of souls." One of Mann's working notes states that it was used to describe Mercury—the Roman equivalent of Hermes, the god who conducted souls to the underworld in Greek mythology. Tadzio thus seems to be a messenger or a guide who announces or leads Aschenbach to his death. He is hardly as threatening as the wanderer, but thanks to their similar postures of propped hands and crossed feet, they resemble each other and the wanderer likewise seems to embody this ancient god. Their pose also recalls the one struck by the handsome youth who, for the ancient Greeks, represented death. This figure is described in *Wie die Alten den Tod gebildet* (How the Ancients Represented Death, 1769), an essay by Gotthold Ephraim Lessing (1729–81). Lessing was a German author whose works Mann knew. In contrast to these two characters who stand, Aschenbach sits. He does so most comfortably when being rowed by the rude gondolier. As Mann writes, gondolas have the softest and most relaxing seats in the world. He also observes, twice, that they are as black as coffins. Sitting and death thus seem related. As noted earlier, in remarks on decadence, the soft seat of the gondola also makes it easy for Aschenbach to give up trying to enforce his will, to get the gondolier to take him where he wants to go. Sitting indicates his loss of willpower at other decisive moments in the novella as well. At the end of the street singers' last number, for example, he no longer rests easily in his chair, his sense of music paralyzed by passion. Instead, he sits upright, as if he were trying to defend himself or to flee. The laughter, the medicinal smell, and Tadzio's proximity all cast their spell, however, and he remains seated long into the night. In fact, Mann hints at Aschenbach's loss of willpower by having him sit at the end of each of the last three chapters. At the end of chapter 3, he is sitting in an armchair at the open window of his hotel room. At the end of chapter 4, he throws himself onto a bench in the park behind the hotel. At the end of chapter 5, before being taken to his room, he rests on his chaise longue at the beach. His head lies on the back of this chair as he watches Tadzio wade into the sea. Again he tries to get up, and again he fails, this time falling over sideways in his chair. At the end of all these chapters, then, Aschenbach sees Tadzio and sits. It seems that he cannot stand, a physical fact that indicates a psychological one: neither can he withstand the power of his passion. The ends of these chapters also show how that passion progresses. Initially, he sees Tadzio from a distance, then the unexpected sight of the boy is overwhelming, and in the end he collapses. Like their clothing, the posture of Mann's characters is thus a motif, a narrative element that has a tale to tell.

Motifs can also be themes or ideas. Three such motifs characterize Aschenbach: falseness, isolation, and belatedness. Mann mentions falseness in the initial paragraph of his story. He refers to the unusually warm weather in Munich, where it is only the beginning of May, as a "falscher Hochsommer" (false high summer). The old man on the boat is likewise "falsch"—that is, not as young as he looks—as Aschenbach remarks with horror. Aschenbach is similarly disgusted by this old man's drunkenness, which results from his "falsche Gemeinschaft" (false association) with the young clerks from Pola. Aschenbach, as noted above, is later made up and dressed to look like this same man. When he looks in the mirror after the barber finishes applying cosmetics, in fact, he sees himself in the bloom of youth. Mann here uses the same word, *Jüngling* (young man), that he earlier used to describe the old fop as "false." The motif of falseness thus links these two aging men in their vain pursuit of youth. Mann also observes several times that Aschenbach is isolated. In the very first sentence of the novella, Aschenbach has gone for a walk alone; in the second paragraph, he takes paths that lead him farther and farther away from other people in the park; and in the third paragraph, he finds the streetcar stop deserted. His isolation thus is stressed from the beginning. He no longer seems to like it, since he fears being alone with his maid and his servant in his summerhouse. Mann reports that his hero grew up in isolation, too. Prevented for medical reasons from attending school, he had no comrades. Later, he assumes the stern manners of a solitude full of suffering and of struggle. This solitude also gains him power and respect. Mann's psychological insight about the mixed blessings of solitude has already been noted. He there remarks on the observations of "des Einsam-Stummen" (the solitary, silent person). He similarly calls his hero "der Einsam-Wache" (the solitary, alert person) or simply "der Einsame" (the solitary). Throughout the novella, then—indeed, throughout his life—Aschenbach is solitary, alone, and isolated. A third motif that characterizes him is belatedness. When he wonders if his decision to leave Venice has been hasty, Mann says, and Aschenbach himself appears to think, the words "Too late." The same two words recur, twice, after Aschenbach tries in vain to speak with Tadzio. This time, Mann emphasizes them with an exclamation point—"Zu spät!" (Too late!)—and clearly indicates that Aschenbach thinks them. This repetition reinforces the theme of belatedness, and this theme in turn helps explain Aschenbach's problem: it seems simply too late for him to lead a new and different life.

Another motif that often recurs in *Death in Venice* is foreignness. It takes several forms and is signaled by the word *fremd* (foreign, strange). First, it links the series of foreign-looking strangers that culminates in Dionysus. The wanderer's straw hat lends him an air of foreignness, and Mann calls him a foreigner. He does not seem at all of Bavarian, the gondolier not at all of Italian, and the street singer not at all of Venetian stock. The mob in Aschenbach's orgiastic dream, moreover, celebrates the arrival of "der fremde Gott" (the foreign god). Aschenbach is honestly willing to protect himself against this foreigner, Mann notes, but is soon enthralled to him. This god, Dionysus, comes from India, as does the cholera epidemic. Second, the motif of foreignness shows a peculiar psychological topography, a mental map of Aschenbach's—and perhaps of Mann's—world. The English clerk, Mann observes, has a loyal nature that is very foreign in the cunning South. After repeating the official line that the hygienic measures being taken in Venice are no cause for alarm, moreover, this clerk raises his blue eyes, which meet "dem Blicke des Fremden" (the gaze of the foreigner). This "foreigner" is Aschenbach, who is not native to Venice. Mann also mentions that he has external traits of a foreign race. These traits come from his mother, the daughter of a Bohemian bandleader. Thus, to Aschenbach, the East and the South, India and Italy, both seem foreign. He is either a foreigner or looks somewhat foreign himself, however, both at home and abroad. What is more, foreignness is something that he wants. He seeks the foreign, as Mann notes at the beginning of chapter 3, and later recalls his youthful yearning, back at the cemetery, for the faraway and the foreign. Third, Mann links the motif of foreignness to language. Aschenbach hears many languages. On the Adriatic island where he initially vacations, the local peasants speak in "wildfremden Lauten" (wild foreign sounds); the musicians in the boat that waylays his first gondola fill the air with their "Fremdenpoesie" (foreign poetry); and at the beach, the "Fremdheit" (foreignness) of Tadzio's speech makes it, to Aschenbach, seem like music. Like these three instances of foreign language, the foreign in *Death in Venice* is at once wild, disturbing, and desired. Fourth, foreignness pervades Venice. Near the end of the novella, Aschenbach sees foreigners who are ignorant of the epidemic. Soon, Mann adds that one seldom sees such foreigners anymore. They are all tourists, and it is the tourist industry that the corrupt Venetian authorities want to save. The word that Mann uses to describe this industry—*Fremdengewerbe*—contains the adjective *fremd* and underscores the foreignness on which Venice so greedily thrives. The motif of foreignness is thus complex. Given these four different forms that it takes, one might say that it makes Aschenbach's love for Tadzio a thoroughly foreign affair.

Like Mann's motifs, two of his narrative techniques are related to the concept of doubling or repetition. The first of these techniques is his foreshadowing of events that occur later in his story. The second is his raising readers' expectations only to postpone their fulfillment. Three examples show how foreshadowing works. While Aschenbach waits at the streetcar stop in Munich, he sees the crosses, headstones, and monuments for sale at the stonemasons' shops. These items suggest the idea of death that becomes so important in the novella. When Aschenbach's ship from Pola approaches Venice, it must stop in the lagoon until it passes a medical inspection. This inspection raises the issue of public sanitation and its enforcement by Venetian officials, an issue that turns out to be crucial during the cholera epidemic. When Mann describes Aschenbach and his family, he mentions that his hero never had a son. This seems a strange detail, one that appears irrelevant at the time Mann mentions it. When Aschenbach first watches Tadzio at the beach, however, he feels paternally inclined to him. His affection for the boy thus initially includes the feelings of a father for a son. None of these three details seems significant until later, in fact, when their relevance to Mann's story turns out to be obvious. Four examples demonstrate how Mann raises and postpones fulfilling his readers' expectations. After Aschenbach first sees Tadzio in the hotel lobby, the other hotel guests go into the dining room. Tadzio turns around before he enters, and their eyes meet. This mutual glance may lead one to expect that Aschenbach will be able to observe the boy more closely at dinner, but his table is very far from that of the Polish family. At breakfast the next morning, though, he is seated just two tables away. Eyes play a similar role in two other examples. Given Aschenbach's growing interest in the boy, one might expect him to betray some sign of his emotion. As Mann says near the end of chapter 4, however, nothing in Aschenbach's cultured and dignified mien does so, even when their gazes sometimes meet. Two paragraphs later, when Tadzio comes home one evening, Aschenbach has no time to make his mien look calm and dignified, and it openly displays joy, surprise, and admiration as his gaze meets Tadzio's. When Aschenbach and Tadzio are located near each other at the street singers' performance, the older man likewise keeps his glances in check at first, and Tadzio, as Mann puts it, cannot find his eyes. After the last song, though, Aschenbach dares to look at the boy, who earnestly looks back. Mann also postpones fulfilling expectations he raises in the scene with the gondolier. When this sinister figure does not take Aschenbach to Saint Mark's, Aschenbach relaxes and thinks the man will have ferried him well, even if he sends him to Hades by hitting him from behind with his oar. This sudden thought of the underworld inhabited by souls of the dead in Greek mythology appears odd. As Mann adds, nothing of the kind occurs. Eventually, of course, Aschenbach does die in Venice, so the gondolier turns out to have played the role of Charon, the mythological boatman who ferried such souls across the River Styx to Hades. Like his repetitions as well as his motifs, then, these two techniques show how tightly Mann's text is woven.

SYMBOLS AND IMAGES

Mann's narrative art also includes symbols and images. A symbol is something that stands for something else. A concrete object, for example, may typify or represent an abstract quality or idea: a lion is a symbol of strength. Such an object and idea may actually be similar, or they may merely be conventionally associated. An image, too, is something that is like something else. Literary images evoke a mental picture, often by using figures of speech such as similes and metaphors, which draw explicit and implicit comparisons, respectively. Symbols and images, then, are related devices. Mann uses both. Sometimes, he even calls them symbols. In chapter 2, for example, he maintains that Saint Sebastian is the symbol of Aschenbach's art. He recalls how a critic once said that the fictional heroes Aschenbach prefers all display a manliness that endures swords and spears piercing its body. Saint Sebastian was a Christian martyr killed in much this way. Aschenbach's art is like him, Mann implies, in that it, too, shows composure when confronted by fate, and grace when being tortured. Such are the virtues of Aschenbach's heroes, such are his own, and such are those of the exhausted moralists of achievement for whom he speaks. Similarly, in chapter 5, the celebrants in Aschenbach's dream hoist what Mann calls "das obszöne Symbol" (the obscene symbol). By this he seems to mean the thyrsus, a staff wrapped in ivy and tipped with a pine cone. He calls this symbol of Dionysus huge and wooden, and he seems to regard it as obscene because it resembles a phallus. That it should thus represent a penis makes sense insofar as Dionysus was a god not only of wine but also of fertility. It suggests, then, that Aschenbach's dream is sexual. The import of some of Mann's images or symbols is clearer than that of others. When Aschenbach remains seated after the street singers finish performing, one reads that there was an hourglass in his parents' house many years ago and that he sees it in his imagination, as if it were standing in front of him. The sand runs silently out of the top bulb and swiftly through the neck. The meaning of this symbol seems clear: time is running out. Aschenbach loses track of time on the boat to Venice, moreover, and stops paying attention to how long he meant to be on vacation. When he is at sea, Mann says that one has no sense of time in an empty, undivided space. Now Mann adds that time disintegrates. The hourglass, then, not only suggests that Aschenbach's life will soon be over. It also is an image tied to an idea that Mann suggests with these other remarks on time: that being and time are related, that being aware of the passage of time is staying alert and alive. By contrast, the camera abandoned in the last scene seems cryptic. It is apparently lordless, as Mann says, and it stands on a tripod at the edge of the sea. A black cloth spread over it flutters clappingly in the colder wind. Photographers are artists, of course, but does the absence of such a "lord" suggest that Aschenbach's days as an artist are over? A tripod was used in relating the prophecies of Apollo, so does the camera confirm that Aschenbach is no longer Apollinian in the sense that Nietzsche defines in *The Birth of Tragedy?* Black is traditionally a color of mourning, but does the black cloth here stand for Aschenbach's imminent death? The camera may mean none of these things, all of them, some of them, or others. Precisely what it symbolizes, if anything, is difficult to say. Imprecision may be a virtue here, however, since it leaves room for interpretation.

Hands, teeth, the weather, and the sea in Mann's story seem especially symbolic. An astute observer, Mann notes, made a fist to show how tensely Aschenbach lived. To show how Aschenbach never relaxed, this observer let his open hand hang comfortably from the arm of his chair. At the end of chapter 3, sitting at the window of his new hotel room, Aschenbach slowly turns and lifts his arms, which hang loosely over those of his chair, turning the palms of his hands outward, as if he were indicating an opening and expansion of his arms. Mann calls this gesture welcoming and receptive. The change in Aschenbach's attitude—his willingness to relax now and an openness to his passion for Tadzio—is conveyed by this symbolic gesture. Teeth are likewise symbols of something greater than themselves. Mann has several characters show them. The wanderer's short lips reveal his long white teeth, the gondolier exposes his similarly white teeth, and the street singer's smile reveals his strong ones. These figures are robust, even menacingly vital. Less threatening but still full of life is the Russian family, whose males have large teeth. At the beach, this family seems to enjoy life. It also enjoys the performance of the street singer. In the first of these scenes, these Russians sit in front of the last cabanas on the left. In the second, they sit in the garden, nearer to the singers than the other guests are on the terrace. In both, they position themselves at the end or at the edge of society, partaking of the more refined as well as the more vigorous world. They there appear to strike and symbolize a balance between extremes that tear Aschenbach apart. This may be why Mann often calls them "dankbar" (thankful). By contrast, Tadzio's teeth do not look healthy. Jagged, pale, and transparent, they inspire Aschenbach's idea that Tadzio is delicate, sickly, and unlikely to grow old. The weather is symbolic, too. In Munich, it is sultry and stormy. Mann thus anticipates Aschenbach's torrid, tempestuous passion. The sky is gray and the wind is damp during the boat ride to Venice, and although the rain stops, the sky and sea remain dreary and leaden. That Mann notes the color gray, then alludes to it with the word *bleiern* (leaden), seems significant, since his hero is graying at the temples. The first word

Aschenbach mutters before the barber starts to rejuvenate him, moreover, is "grau" (gray). The weather is no better on the morning after he arrives, and he remembers how it once made him leave Venice. The sun shines and the sky shimmers at the beginning of chapter 4, but by the end of chapter 5 a stormy wind is blowing. Throughout *Death in Venice*, the weather thus mirrors Aschenbach's moods. His love of the sea and its simple enormity, its undivided nothingness, has been noted already, as has the idea that the sea suggests nirvana, a Buddhistic state of bliss. Mann also describes life at the beach as culture on the verge of the element and thus hints at another symbolic meaning of the sea: as nature, it contrasts with the civilized behavior and the intellectual and artistic efforts—that is, with the culture—that weigh on Aschenbach.

One of Mann's most telling images is the city of Venice. This city is symbolic in his story because its attributes seem both literal and figurative. In certain ways, it also corresponds to his hero. Aschenbach, having decided to leave Venice, takes a gondola to Saint Mark's Square, but the gondolier tries to make him stop and buy things along the way. The spell cast by his strange ride is thus broken by the mercenary spirit "der gesunkenen Königin" (of the sunken queen). This phrase has more than one meaning. Venice has long been known as "the queen of the seas," and it has sunken both in the sense that many of its structures, built on wooden pilings that rot, are slipping below the surface of the water, and in the sense that it has lost the maritime power that was once the source of its wealth. When Aschenbach takes another gondola, in pursuit of Tadzio, Mann makes a further remark about this city. It is a flattering and a dubious beauty, he writes, half fairy tale and half tourist trap. Among the things Aschenbach sees in this scene are fragrant flowers that hang over crumbling walls. Venice is both literally and figuratively decadent, then, decaying physically as well as morally. It is also a labyrinth. In these scenes involving gondolas, Mann calls the famous canals of Venice a labyrinth. When Aschenbach later loses his way, the entire city seems to be such a confusing place. Literally, labyrinths are just such places, ones like the maze Daedalus built to confine the child-eating Minotaur. Figuratively, a labyrinth is an intricate, confusing difficulty or affair. Aschenbach is caught in both kinds, both in a complicated system of waterways, alleys, bridges, and squares, and in an emotional entanglement. The labyrinthine nature of Venice also relates this city to the tropical landscape that Aschenbach envisions in Munich. That imaginary landscape, too, is a swamp with islands and channels. As noted earlier, it also resembles the delta of the Ganges River, which the English clerk describes as the origin of the cholera epidemic in India. Venice is thus linked to this second, actual tropical landscape as well. The image of a labyrinth, then, makes Venice seem a veritable jungle of a city. Mann also calls this city sick, personifying it as if it were a patient like those dying in its hospitals. Cases of cholera have been occurring there ever since Aschenbach left Munich in the middle of May, so sanitary conditions in Venice seem to parallel his journey. Mann notes that the adventure of the outside world, the unclean events going on in the city, coincides with that of Aschenbach's heart and feeds his passion with hope. Later, Mann observes that Aschenbach suffers fits of dizziness accompanied by a feeling that there is no way out and no hope. It is unclear, Mann says, whether this feeling has to do with the external world or with Aschenbach's own life. This ambiguity confirms how intimately the city of Venice and Aschenbach are related.

Mann's symbols and images are in turn linked to the way in which he combines psychology and myth. Most of his various references and allusions to Greek myths are noted in the summary of his plot given earlier. In chapter 4, for example, he expressly refers to Helios, the sun god; Elysium, where the blessed dwelled happily after death; Zeus and his abduction of Ganymede, a beautiful shepherd boy; Eros, the god of love; Eos, the goddess of dawn, and four men she seduced; Poseidon, the god of the sea; Pan, a god of fertility; Hyacinth, the beautiful boy killed when Zephyr, the god of the west wind, blew Apollo's discus off course; and Narcissus, the beautiful youth who died for love after becoming enamored of his own reflection. In chapter 5, Aschenbach senses the presence of Harpies, mythical monsters shaped like birds. As noted earlier, most of these references or allusions to Greek myths have erotic connotations and thus suggest that the love story Mann tells is poetic as well as antique. To the extent that they occur to Aschenbach himself, and not just to Mann, they also show what he has read, hinting that he received a classical education. In this respect, they resemble his recollections of passages from Homer, Plato, Xenophon, and Plutarch. They also betray how he views and justifies his interest in Tadzio, which he casts in terms borrowed from mythology. Three other instances in which Mann uses such terms have been noted in this chapter: the gondolier conveys Aschenbach in a way reminiscent of Charon, the boatman who ferried the souls of the dead to Hades; the word *panic* connotes Pan and thus links mythology, sexuality, and disease; and the wanderer and Tadzio function as Hermes, the god who conducted souls to the underworld. These three examples show Mann telling his story on two levels at once. On one level, the events of that story occur in its fictional world, which neatly parallels the actual world of Munich and Venice that existed in the early twentieth century. On the other level, these events echo or repeat actions taken in the world of Greek mythology. Two other events similarly take place on both these levels. Both those events involve drinking. When Aschenbach goes to lunch on the boat to Venice, it turns out that the clerks have been drinking with the captain since ten in the morning. When these young men come on deck and cheer the Italian sharpshooters who are drilling in Venice, they are enthused by Asti, an Italian white wine. Dionysus was the Greek god of wine, so even this seemingly minor scene underscores the concept of the Dionysian in *Death in Venice*. As Aschenbach listens to the street singers, moreover, he sips from his glass of pomegranate juice and soda water. A pomegranate is a reddish fruit, and there is no reason why its juice should not be in Aschenbach's drink. A pomegranate, though, is also the fruit whose seeds the young Greek goddess Persephone was tricked into eating by Hades or Pluto, the god of the underworld. Like the gondolier, this seemingly minor detail is thus subtly infernal. This duality of Mann's narration has been characterized as "myth plus psychology." He thereby encompasses both the real and the transcendent, it is said, and lends the realistic details of his story symbolic meaning.[1]

POINTS OF VIEW

In addition to verbs and nouns, diverse repetition, and symbols and images, the narrative art of *Death in Venice* includes subtle handling of two or three points of view. One of these points of view is Aschenbach's; another is Mann's. There may be a third: that of Mann's implied narrator. Aschenbach is a fictional character, Mann is an actual, real-life author, and the narrator is an unnamed persona. Their respective angles on the events of the novella sometimes seem markedly different. Many of those events, for example, are related from Aschenbach's perspective. What actually happens, in fact, is often hard to determine since Mann often narrates only what seems, to Aschenbach, to occur. Indeed, two of the most frequent and most important phrases in *Death in Venice* are "es schien" (it seemed) and "ihm war, als ob . . ." (To him, [it] was as if . . .). Many of the most crucial scenes contain them. In chapter 1, the wanderer wears significant items of clothing, *as it seems*, and his lips, which show his long white teeth, *seem* too short. The passage in Aschenbach's writing that has stymied him *seems* to resist all his attempts to fix it, and it *seems* to him as if his work lacks verve. Both the reason for his walk and the stranger he sees on it thus appear to be narrated from Aschenbach's own point of view. In chapter 3, it *seems* he should not rest too much in the gondola; the hotel guests *seem* predominantly Slavic; Tadzio's sisters, between fifteen and seventeen years old, *as it seems, seem* kempt and attired according stricter rules than he is; women *seem* worried that Tadzio is too far out in the sea; and *it almost seems* to Aschenbach that he is at the beach to protect the boy. Aschenbach's sense of danger as well as the attention that he pays to Slavs, Poles, and Tadzio in particular are both, then, narrated from his less and less impartial perspective. In chapter 4, Aschenbach retires early, since the day, *to him, seems* over when Tadzio leaves the scene. In chapter 5, it *has seemed to him as if* Tadzio's posture and breathing during the street singers' performance are signs of his sickliness, and when he stares at Tadzio and follows him through the streets, the monstrous *seems* promising, the moral law invalid. Other constructions similarly hint that Mann relates the events of *Death in Venice* through Aschenbach's increasingly infatuated eyes. In the final scene, for example, Aschenbach is watching Tadzio, who is standing on a sandbar and suddenly turns and looks at the beach. Aschenbach sits as he was sitting when the boy's gaze first met his, cast from the threshold of the dining room at the hotel. *To him, it is as if* the pale and lovely psychagogue were smiling and waving at him, *as if* he were pointing out, hovering ahead into the promising and the enormous. By repeating "as if" here, Mann makes it plain that readers see this image only as it appears to Aschenbach. Tadzio may not actually be a psychagogue, a conductor of souls, and thus like Hermes. He may not be smiling or waving at Aschenbach and may not be pointing or hovering. This is simply how the dying Aschenbach perceives him. Like Aschenbach's vision of a tropical landscape, this scene may be a daydream—meaningful, but hallucinatory. One must therefore read this scene very carefully. As in all of *Death in Venice*, Mann is often describing only his ailing hero's subjective impressions, not the objective fictional facts.

There is another way in which Mann indicates that some of his story is narrated from Aschenbach's point of view. This second way involves the notion of free indirect discourse. Such discourse consists of words that are written by an author or a narrator reporting a fictional character's thoughts but that appear to come from that character's point of view. Such free indirect discourse is in the third person and the past tense and the indicative mood. This mood is the form of a verb that denotes a fact. Free indirect discourse lacks an introductory clause such as "She thought, . . .", and it does not put the character's thoughts in quotation marks. *Direct* discourse contains such clauses and quotation marks, as in "He asked him-self, 'Am I crazy?'" *Indirect* discourse contains an introductory clause but lacks quotations marks, often uses the subjunctive mood of the verb, and changes the final punctuation, as in "He asked himself if he were crazy." In *free indirect* discourse, this sentence becomes a question: "Was he crazy?" It may seem that only an author or a narrator could ask such questions, but a character, too, might pose them. One needs to know their context, to read the other text around them. One can then, sometimes, tell who raises them. One cannot always decide, though, whose perspective is be-ing given. In free indirect discourse, then, characters' points of view can subtly tinge the events that an author or narrator reports. Mann employs it often. Several questions suggesting it occur in chapter 3. They often have to do with Tadzio. When Aschenbach realizes that he should be in Venice rather than in his first vacation spot, an unnamed island in the Adriatic Sea, one of Mann's sentences is "Was sollte er hier?" (What was he doing here?). If this question were posed from Mann's own point of view, it would end with the word *there*. The word *here* makes sense only from Aschenbach's perspective. When Aschenbach notices that the fop associating with the clerks on the boat is old, Mann poses another ques-tion: "Wußten, bemerkten sie nicht, daß er alt . . . war?" (Did they not know, not notice, that he was . . . old?). This question makes the most sense if Aschenbach is asking it. When Aschenbach first sees Tadzio's delicate features, one of Mann's sentences is "War er leidend?" (Was he suffering?). It could come directly from Mann, but it makes more sense if it expresses Aschenbach's curiosity. This question is soon followed by another, one that asks if Tadzio is simply pampered. Together, these ques-tions seem to suggest Aschenbach's initial interest in the beautiful boy. Other questions occur as Aschenbach tries to leave Venice. When he wakes up on the morning after he decides to go, the air seems fresher, and he starts to rue his decision. Had it not been hasty and mistaken? En route to the train station, he sees the sights of Venice again. Was it possible that he had not known, not considered how much his heart clung to all these things? On the way back, after he has missed his train, the weather seems better. Was he deceived, or was there really a sea-breeze? All three of these questions make sense from Aschenbach's point of view, for he seems to be asking himself what he was thinking and whether his sense of the wind is reliable. Chapter 4 includes further such questions, and two of them are especially suggestive. What moved Tadzio to start passing in front of Aschenbach's cabana instead of using the boardwalk behind it? Did the attraction, the fascination of a superior feeling, have this effect on its tender and thoughtless object? Aschenbach here seems to assume that Tadzio intentionally passes in front of him and that the boy, whom he seems to regard as thoughtless, does so because he finds Aschenbach's feeling for him attractive, even fascinating. Aschenbach also seems to consider this feeling superior, situated on high. These questions, if asked from Aschenbach's point of view, thus suggest how much he flatters and how highly he regards himself. In fact, Mann may even be inviting readers, at least those who understand free indirect discourse, to see his hero in an ironic light.

Indeed, the concept of irony helps show how Mann sometimes distances himself from Aschenbach. It can also help distinguish his opinion of Aschenbach from that of a more critical narrator. The word *irony* can mean many things. Here, it will be used in a basic sense of "words used to suggest or convey the opposite of their literal meaning." Mann also employs something much like dramatic irony, showing readers more than Aschenbach knows about his own situation. As noted, the first kind of irony may occur in the last question cited in the previous paragraph. Aschenbach's feeling for Tadzio is said to be superior, but this statement could imply its opposite: that his feeling is not at all as superior as Aschenbach himself appears to think. Other instances of irony occur throughout the novella. After Aschenbach hears Tadzio called something like "Adgio," Mann writes that guessing the boy's name seemed, to the earnest man, an appropriate and absorbing task. This statement, though, implies that a man who thinks so is not at all earnest. When Aschenbach believes he sees beauty itself in Tadzio, Mann adds that this is intoxication, which the aging artist unhesitatingly and even greedily welcomes. He also calls him "der Enthusiasmierte" (the enthused), implying that he is possessed. The word *enthused* denotes inspiration by a god. In this case, the god must be Eros. As noted above, Mann mentions "the infatuated's way of thinking." He is referring to Aschenbach's musings about homoeroticism among some military heroes of antiquity. Aschenbach himself does not seem to understand just how intoxicated, enthused, and infatuated he may be. Finally, when Aschenbach sits down in his forlorn square, eats strawberries, and dreams of Plato's *Phaedrus*, Mann writes, "Er saß dort, der Meister, der würdig gewordene Künstler . . . " (He sat there, the master, the dignified artist . . .). Mann then recalls all of Aschenbach's supposed achievements, all the highlights of his career that were recounted in chapter 2. In this scene, though, Aschenbach is hardly a master, he is not at all dignified, and those achievements have turned out to be empty. This last instance of irony is so obvious and so harsh that it may discredit itself. It may be doubly ironic and mean the opposite of its own ironic implication. This possibility exists because one can posit a second narrative voice, that is, a narrator other than Mann himself. Implicitly, *Death in Venice* has such a narrator, who is not necessarily identical with its author. Mann wrote the novella, of course, so this separate narrator is still his creation, but one may need to draw a distinction between them. Mann may not agree with this narrator. Indeed, he may even take an ironic attitude toward this narrator's statements.[2] In the end, then, Mann's opinion of Aschenbach may be like a positive number that results from multiplying two negative ones. If the narrator has a negative view of Aschenbach, and Mann has a negative view of the narrator, then Mann's view of his hero is positive. If the narrator is critical of Aschenbach, and Mann is critical of the narrator, then Mann's opinion of his hero is sympathetic. It may not be possible to decide, for irony is subtle and often ambiguous. Mann's point of view may not differ from his narrator's, and his opinion of his hero may be unfavorable after all. This may be a matter of interpretation, at least for readers who appreciate Mann's narrative art.

NOTES

1. André von Gronicka, "'Myth Plus Psychology': A Style Analysis of *Death in Venice*," *Germanic Review* 31.3 (October 1956): 191–205.

2. Dorrit Cohn, *Transparent Minds: Narrative Modes for Presenting Consciousness in Fiction* (Princeton: Princeton University Press, 1978); Cohn, "The Second Author of 'Der Tod in Venedig,'" in *Probleme der Moderne*, ed. Benjamin Bennett, Anton Kaes, and William J. Lillyman (Tübingen: Niemeyer, 1983), 223–45.

7 Reception

Literary works are often easier to understand when one knows something about their reception, that is, about how critics and scholars have reacted and responded to them. A critic is someone who judges such works, often professionally, often in book reviews. Scholars—academic teachers and researchers—likewise write about such works, using their specialized knowledge. A survey of the critical and scholarly response to *Death in Venice* shows that it can be divided into two phases: first, the years from the initial publication of the novella in 1912 until Mann's death in 1955; second, the years since then. Each of these phases has its particular interests and special emphases, although much in the reception of Mann's story has not varied. A summary of the approaches that critics and scholars have taken to that story demonstrates such shifting interests and emphases, as well as such unchanging elements. Most of the approaches can be classified as genetic, thematic, stylistic, comparative, historical, or psychoanalytical. Adaptations of the novella in other media, too, have attracted critical and scholarly attention. These approaches and this attention, considered together, show just how differently *Death in Venice* has been evaluated and how many different things it has seemed to mean.

THE CRITICAL AND SCHOLARLY RESPONSE

During Mann's life, *Death in Venice* met with a mixed reception before becoming almost universally accepted. In the first two years after its initial publication in the fall of 1912, it was discussed in over forty reviews.

Almost all of them appeared in German, Swiss, or Austrian newspapers or journals. Most were favorable, but although many of their authors admired the novella, some decidedly did not. Indeed, it occasioned some sharply worded exchanges. Some reviewers disliked Mann's theme of pederasty, being either repelled or offended, but others considered this sexual behavior symbolic or not as significant as the language in which he wrote about it. His literary style seemed most important to many. These reviewers liked the composition or form of his story, praising its structure or its prose. Others thought it too cold and conscious, faulting its tone or its hero's temperament. Many reviewers equated Mann with Aschenbach, but others drew distinctions between them. Some criticized Mann's conception of artists generally; a few opposed Aschenbach in particular. Some reviewers were far more judicious than others. Some were clearly personally or politically motivated. At first, then, *Death in Venice* was successful but controversial. Later in Mann's life, it was almost always seen as a classic. This development is partly due to historical and intellectual events that seemed to lend the novella new and urgent meaning. Political readings were common, in part because Aschenbach seemed to embody what was right or wrong with all Germany before and during the First World War, or to represent the irrational tendency leading to National Socialism, or to show what had gone awry in all Western culture. The novella acquired a greater international reputation when it was translated into both English and French in 1924. Mann himself, moreover, often wrote or spoke about it. His comments suggest conflicting intentions and interpretations. He, too, held *Death in Venice* in high regard, but its import seems to have changed with the times for him as well.

After Mann's death in 1955, the reception of the novella became even broader and deeper. Critics and scholars could now consider his life and work as a whole and consult both his archives and his correspondence. Some of their remarks on *Death in Venice* attest to such reflection or research. They also addressed many issues that had been raised during his life, or they broached new subjects and drew new conclusions. As a result, the novella increasingly became the object of academic industry. Renewed interest in it—and greater sales—resulted from Luchino Visconti's film *Morte a Venezia* (1971) and from Benjamin Britten's opera *Death in Venice* (1973). By 1975, in fact, when the hundredth anniversary of Mann's birth was celebrated, its reception seemed both extensive and exhaustive. This fact did not keep critics and scholars from interpreting *Death in Venice* in subsequent years. In 1977, Mann's diaries began to be published. In 1995, three major biographies of him appeared.[1] There were newly accessible personal records to consult, then, and new accounts of his life to consider. Most studies written in these years nonetheless treat the same topics raised in previous ones: Aschenbach's significance as an artist, general or historical issues of art and aesthetics, philosophical concepts, political events, and Mann's allusions to Greek myths. There have been new comparisons drawn between his story and other fiction, moreover, new analyses of his style, and new psychoanalytic commentaries. More critics and scholars now talk about his homoeroticism. Some take a very polemical or provocative tone; others, including Mann's biographers, have expressed different opinions of its emotional significance to him. What sets the last few years apart from prior decades are readings of the novella that stress conflicts between cultures. These readings are inspired by recent theoretical interest taken in orientalism and colonialism, that is, in the perceptions of and political interaction with the East. This is only the latest of the many academic fashions that are reflected in the long, ongoing reception of *Death in Venice*.

CRITICAL AND SCHOLARLY APPROACHES

Some critics and scholars take a genetic approach to the novella. They explain the circumstances in which Mann created it as well as the literary and other written sources he used. Their comments pertain to his personal life, his career, and his erudition, that is, to knowledge he gained from reading those sources. Such comments can explain details of the vacation that took him to Venice in May and June of 1911, including his sighting of a beautiful Polish boy on the beach there. They may also tell how he heard of the death of Gustav Mahler during his trip, and they may mention an essay he wrote then, in which he advocates a new classicality, a manner of art that differs from the romantic operas of Richard Wagner.[2] Genetic studies may also explain how Mann actually composed *Death in Venice* over the course of the following year. They may rely on his correspondence as well as on his working notes to show what he was thinking and how he put the sources quoted in those notes to creative use. His letters suggest that he initially intended *Death in Venice* to be about Goethe, for example, a fact that has often invited speculation about his psychological motives for writing it. Was he trying to disguise his homoerotic urges by claiming that he meant to describe one of Goethe's heterosexual love affairs? Was he trying to do away, vicariously, with this famous literary predecessor and rival? For that matter, is the fact that Aschenbach has written several works that Mann began but then never finished a sign that Mann was trying to overcome an impasse in his own career? Did Mann change his mind while he wrote, only then becoming critical of Aschenbach? These are questions that scholars who take one or another genetic approach have raised. In any case, his notes contain a wealth of information about Aschenbach, Tadzio, Greek mythology, and cholera. His sources include Homer, Plato, Plutarch, Erwin Rohde, and Georg Lukács. Other influences, not mentioned in his notes, include Goethe, Nietzsche, Schopenhauer, and perhaps—though the experts disagree—Euripides and Freud. All of these biographical and philological facts, often indirectly, left traces in Mann's fiction.

Approaches taken by other critics and scholars are thematic. These approaches lead to Mann's subjects and ideas, most notably aestheticism, homoeroticism, and the Dionysian. Studies concerned with aestheticism treat Aschenbach's belief in the value and virtue of art and beauty. They often discuss what kind of artist he is and whether his own, literary art is good or bad. Some admire him as a tragic hero; others call him misguided or even criminal. Some find his writing great; others consider it too forced. These studies also discuss the extent to which Mann shares his hero's aesthetic views. Some argue that he generally agrees with them and that he disowns only the specific consequences that they have for Aschenbach. Others claim that he distances himself from their basic premises, including the idea that all art is sensual. Studies concerned with homoeroticism mention Aschenbach's sexual interest and desire inspired by and directed to members of his own sex. They frequently discuss whether his attraction to Tadzio is damnable, liberating, degrading, or uplifting. Some maintain that any such attraction is immoral or that Aschenbach is particularly corrupted; others say that he frees himself from mistaken notions of proper behavior. Some argue that he loses his status or is humiliated; others suggest that he attains a higher level of consciousness. Earlier, such studies often, though hardly always, displayed distaste. More recently, they tend to be enthusiastic about Aschenbach's supposed sexual preference for men. Studies concerned with the Dionysian explain how Aschenbach exchanges sober self-control for intoxicated abandon. They often note similarities between *Death in Venice* and Nietzsche's *Die Geburt der Tragödie* (The Birth of Tragedy, 1872). They also reach differing conclusions about the "foreign god," Dionysus, worshiped in Aschenbach's dream. Some think letting go of inhibitions, as Aschenbach does, benefits individuals; others think that doing so damages society. These three subjects or ideas are not the only ones raised in *Death in Venice* and discussed in its reception. The others include death, Venice, decadence, visual contact, time, and the names of Mann's characters.

Further approaches to *Death in Venice* are stylistic. Critics and scholars who take them explain either the form in which Mann wrote his story or the manner in which he expresses himself, either the structure of the novella, that is, or the language used in it. Those who study its structure often focus on its narrative organization or arrangement. Divided into five chapters, it is sometimes compared to a tragedy in five acts. It has also often been compared to music. It introduces and recapitulates its themes and motifs, as musical compositions do; it seems to have various tempi; and it reaches a noisy climax. Indeed, Mann's use of motifs—recurring elements—such as falseness or foreignness and his repetition of details such as the traits shared and clothes worn by the wanderer, the gondolier, and the street singer have prompted comparisons with Wagner's techniques of musical composition. Other structural issues are irony, narrative voice, and point of view. The novella sounds ironic when Mann calls the delirious Aschenbach a "master." Aschenbach's mania hardly warrants such praise, and Mann actually seems critical or even mocking. This statement has been attributed to a narrator, though, to a narrative voice distinct from that of Mann, the actual author. For that matter, most of the crucial events in the novella are related from Aschenbach's point of view, often in free indirect discourse. As noted earlier, such discourse subtly introduces a character's perspective. In fact, these events may occur only in his imagination. Distinguishing Mann from his hero, and maybe from his narrator, is therefore crucial to figuring out what happens in his fictional world. It also helps readers determine if Mann is sympathetic or hostile to Aschenbach—or if he is ambivalent. Critics and scholars who study the language of *Death in Venice* often note its images or symbols. The tiger and the jungle in the vision that Aschenbach has near the cemetery in Munich, for example, seem to stand for his dangerous desire and emotional morass. Mann's prose is often written in hexameters, moreover, a poetic meter recalling epics of ancient Greece, the mythical land to which Aschenbach feels transported. Similarly, Mann starts by using stiff syntax and diction, choosing and ordering words as Aschenbach would; later, he writes in a more flowing or flowery way. Both his prose and his hero thus become more relaxed. This shift, too, shows how well his style suits his story.

Comparative approaches to *Death in Venice* treat it together with other literary works, citing similarities and differences. Those other works are either by Mann or by other authors. Critics and scholars who compare the novella and Mann's other works often note recurrences and variations of its important themes: progressive decadence, symbolic disease, repressed sexual desire, artists' morality, the ethics of aestheticism, the emotional burden of playing a public role, the psychic cost of asceticism, and the difficulty of transcending knowledge to achieve what Mann called "wiedergeborene Unbefangenheit" (reborn naiveté). Comparisons of *Death in Venice* with Mann's other writings also mention his subsequent use of ancient myths, especially that of Hermes, and his treatment of episodes in the life and works of Goethe, episodes other than the biographical one that he claimed he initially meant the novella to treat. These several themes and methods also occur in his other novellas, his novels, and his only play, as well as in his speeches, essays, and other nonfiction. One example not cited above, in chapter 1, is *Die Betrogene* (The Deceived Woman, translated as The Black Swan, 1953). This story is about a menopausal woman who, like Aschenbach, conceives a final and fatal passion for a handsome young man. Critics and scholars who compare *Death in Venice* with the works of other authors likewise cite other occurrences of its themes or narrative techniques. Such works include Mann's sources as well as other texts, some written earlier than his novella, others later. Foremost among them are Euripides' *The Bacchae*, Goethe's *Die Wahlverwandtschaften* (Elective Affinities, 1809), Joseph Conrad's *Heart of Darkness* (1899), and André Gide's *L'immoraliste* (The Immoralist, 1902). Like these four texts, most of the others to which his story is compared come from Europe. Many were written in one of the German-speaking countries: Germany, Austria, or Switzerland. Thanks to its translations into more than thirty languages, however, that story is now known all over the world. New comparative readings thus seem likely.

Other critics and scholars approach *Death in Venice* historically. They interpret it in the context of past events. Some of the events they mention are literary, whereas others are social or political. The literary events include the ebb and flow of movements such as romanticism, aestheticism, decadence, symbolism, naturalism, and neoclassicism. Mann and Aschenbach have seemed either their representatives or their critics. Some scholars locate *Death in Venice* in the history of the novella as a modern or a German literary genre. They often call it an ultimate, supreme example of this kind of fiction. Social and political events linked to Mann's story include the deeds of Frederick the Great, the First World War, National Socialism, and the Prussian or Protestant ethic. Aschenbach's complex similarities to Frederick are noted above, in chapter 4; so are implications of his coming from Silesia, a province that Frederick conquered. Several details of *Death in Venice* tied to historical conflicts preceding the First World War are also cited there. During that war, Aschenbach seemed to stand for the German nation, for both its social malaise and its military discipline. Depending on a given critic's or scholar's point of view, he displayed either symptoms of cultural decline or heroic and soldierly resolve. Some thought his conservatism the way of the future, while others consigned it to the past. During the Second World War—as noted, again in chapter 4—Georg Lukács argued that Aschenbach represented an ethic of composure that typified the bourgeoisie in late nineteenth- and early twentieth-century Germany. Lukács also observed that Mann shows this ethic to be hollow. Other, often far less subtle, Marxist critics similarly thought Mann's hero symbolic of Prussia and its supposedly barbaric, prefascistic bourgeoisie. More general studies assert that he typifies what is wrong with Western civilization or all bourgeois culture. Others tell how Mann incorporated historical details and how he portrays Poland. Finally, Aschenbach has also seemed to represent the Protestant ethic that the sociologist Max Weber thought had encouraged the spirit of capitalism. These historical approaches often reflect concerns of their day. Such concerns can soon seem dated, but they can also heighten one's appreciation of *Death in Venice,* and they help explain why each generation of readers has found in it something new.

A further kind of approach to *Death in Venice* is psychoanalytical. The critics and scholars who take it use notions suggested by Freud and others to analyze unconscious elements or levels in the mind of Aschenbach or Mann. Some professional psychoanalysts do so as well; others report how the novella has affected their patients. These critics, scholars, and doctors often argue that Aschenbach pays a high price for repressing his unfulfilled sexual desires, which return with a vengeance in his hallucinations and his dreams. They also often contend that Mann must have been working through crises or otherwise coming to terms with his own psychic tensions, including Oedipal conflicts. Some discuss Aschenbach's or Mann's primal scenes, sexual and destructive instincts, sublimations, and defense mechanisms. These authors invoke not only Freud but also Carl Gustav Jung (1875–1961). Psychoanalysts who tell how their patients react to *Death in Venice* often note how it either occasions or helps them overcome problems in their mental or emotional lives. These various kinds of psychoanalytical readings can be illuminating. After all, Aschenbach has dismissed what Mann calls "unanständiger Psychologismus" (indecent psychologism). This fictional fact positively seems to invite interpretations of indecent thoughts that he has suppressed. Such interpretations often seem amateurish, however, thanks to their authors' lack of professional expertise. Many literary critics or scholars have no formal training in psychoanalysis. They therefore often appear merely to dabble in it and either to misunderstand or to misapply its basic concepts. Practicing psychoanalysts, moreover, usually lack formal literary training. As a result, they often fail to grasp the implications of subtle linguistic and narrative techniques. Accordingly, Aschenbach's psyche and Mann's storytelling alike are very often misconstrued. It is a striking fact, though, that articles about *Death in Venice* are regularly published not only in literary journals but also in scientific ones devoted to the study of psychoanalysis.

In addition to being approached in these various ways, *Death in Venice* has been adapted in other media. Critics and scholars sometimes comment on these adaptations, most often on Visconti's film or Britten's opera. Those who regard the former often note how this cinematic version of Aschenbach's story differs from Mann's text. Some reject it because it departs from that text in so many ways. For example, Visconti begins with Mann's third chapter, omitting the first two, which help explain Aschenbach's reasons for going to Venice and his attraction to Tadzio's beauty. In the film, moreover, he is a composer, rather than a writer. This change in his profession is a problem, since music, according to Nietzsche, is the art of Dionysus. Mann's "Apollinian" Aschenbach yields to the spell of this "foreign god" only gradually. Linking Aschenbach with music from the outset, then, fundamentally changes the sense of Mann's story. Another objection is that Visconti makes Aschenbach seem lewd and Tadzio look seductive, thereby losing Mann's psychological and intellectual scope. Others critics and scholars maintain that fiction and film are very different arts and that Visconti's many alterations are justified. More than a few have overlooked these changes, wrongly assuming that what Visconti shows is what Mann wrote. By contrast, Britten's opera is almost always described as successful and equivalent to Mann's story. Among other things, all of its sinister male characters, and even the god Dionysus, are sung by the same voice. This circumstance conveys their relatedness. Furthermore, rather than speak, its Tadzio dances. *Death in Venice* has also been performed as a ballet, in fact, most notably one choreographed by Flemming Flindt and starring Rudolf Nureyev as Aschenbach. There are plays ringing further changes on Mann's novella, and paintings and drawings depicting it.[3] *Death in Venice* has not only busied critics and scholars, then, but inspired many creative artists as well. Their efforts, too, are part of its reception.

NOTES

1. Klaus Harpprecht, *Thomas Mann: Eine Biographie* ([Reinbek bei Hamburg:] Rowohlt, 1995); Ronald Hayman, *Thomas Mann: A Biography* (New York:

Scribner, 1995); Donald Prater, *Thomas Mann: A Life* (Oxford: Oxford University Press, 1995).

2. *Über die Kunst Richard Wagners* (On the Art of Richard Wagner, 1911).

3. For example, Lee Breuer, *A Prelude to Death in Venice* (New York: Plays in Process, 1980); *Der Tod in Venedig: Hommage à Thomas Mann et Luchino Visconti: Zeichnungen, Aquarelle und Gemälde von Jörg Madlener [und] Jan Vanriet* (Darmstadt: Kunstverein Darmstadt, 1978); Joan Waddell, "Two Illustrations for Death in Venice," *Trend* 1.2 (February 1942): 15–17.

8   Bibliographical Essay

Hundreds of books, articles, and reviews have been written about *Death in Venice*. This chapter treats the most important studies of the novella, briefly describing their topics. It groups them according to the six categories used in chapter 7 to order the critical and scholarly approaches to the novella: genetic, thematic, stylistic, comparative, historical, and psychoanalytical. Like that chapter, it also regards critics' and scholars' remarks on adaptations of the novella in other media. Facts of publication are included, so readers can consult these studies on their own for further details. Like the survey of critics' and scholars' responses and the summary of their approaches given in the previous chapter, this selection and description of secondary literature helps show all that has been made of Mann's story and where further research can lead. For a full discussion of the sources cited here, see Ellis Shookman, *Thomas Mann's Death in Venice: A Novella and Its Critics* (Rochester, NY: Camden House, 2003).

GENETIC STUDIES

Josef Hofmiller, "Thomas Manns neue Erzählung," *Süddeutsche Monatshefte* 10 (May 1913): 218–32, posits that a mental and emotional liberation as well as an erotic encounter prompted Mann to write the novella. This fine study also notes structural and stylistic features such as its symbolic characters and its hexametric prose. In his *Lebensabriß* (Life-Sketch, 1930), Mann himself cites symbolic details of his vacation in Venice in 1911 that recur in his story. The biography that describes those details most thoroughly, and that makes the most complete attempt to interpret the novella in light of them, is Peter de Mendelssohn, *Der Zauberer: Das Leben des deutschen Schriftstellers Thomas Mann* (Frankfurt am Main: Fischer, 1975). Regarding the novella as Mann's hypothetical autobiography, T. J. Reed, *Thomas Mann: The Uses of Tradition* (Oxford: Clarendon, 1974), contends that Mann tempered his originally hymnic impulse and wrote a moral fable instead, with ambiguous results. This argument, together with Mann's working notes and with other bibliographical aids, can also be found in the definitive edition of *Death in Venice*, namely *Thomas Mann: Der Tod in Venedig*, ed. T. J. Reed (Munich: Hanser, 1983). Aschenbach's strong similarity, as an artist, to Richard Wagner—whose autobiography appeared in 1911, the year in which Mann started to write his novella—is noted in Werner Vortriede, "Richard Wagners 'Tod in Venedig,'" *Euphorion*, Dritte Folge, 52 (1958): 378–96. Similar resemblances between Aschenbach and the poet August von Platen, who wrote sonnets in Venice about sites and feelings that also figure in Mann's story, are explained in Joachim Seyppel, "Adel des Geistes: Thomas Mann und August von Platen," *Deutsche Vierteljahrsschrift für Literaturwissenschaft und Geistesgeschichte* 33 (1959): 565–73. One can learn how Mann adapted passages from Erwin Rohde's *Psyche* (1890–94) and how this book about the Greeks' cult of the soul and belief in immortality awakened Mann's interest in myth in Herbert Lehnert, "Thomas Mann's Early Interest in Myth and Erwin Rohde's *Psyche*" *PMLA* 79.3 (June 1964): 297–304. Manfred Dierks, *Studien zu Mythos und Psychologie bei Thomas Mann* (Bern: Francke, 1972), likewise explains Mann's use of myth, arguing that he found in Nietzsche's *The Birth of Tragedy* both the idea for his "Apollinian" hero and a model for his story: Euripides' *The Bacchae*. One of several studies that examine his debt to Georg Lukács—especially to Lukács's essay *Sehnsucht und Form* (Yearning and Form, 1911), which discusses the concept of love defined in Plato's *Phaedrus* and *Symposium*—is Judith Marcus-Tar, *Thomas Mann und Georg Lukács* (Cologne: Böhlau, 1982). Mann's allusions to Greek texts such as Xenophon's *Memorabilia* and Homer's *Odyssey* lend his story multiple dimensions, according to Werner Deuse, "'Besonders ein antikisierendes Kapitel scheint mir gelungen': Griechisches in *Der Tod in Venedig*," in *"Heimsuchung und süßes Gift": Erotik und Poetik bei Thomas Mann*, ed. Gerhard Härle, 41–62 (Frankfurt am Main: Fischer, 1992). The origins of *Death in Venice* lie in Mann's plan to write a work like Goethe's *Faust*, with which his novella competes, maintains Werner Frizen, "Der 'Drei-Zeilen Plan' Thomas Manns: Zur Vorgeschichte von *Der Tod in Venedig*," *Thomas Mann Jahrbuch* 5 (1992):

125–41; "Fausts Tod in Venedig," in *Wagner—Nietzsche—Thomas Mann: Festschrift für Eckhard Heftrich*, ed. Heinz Gockel, Michael Neumann, and Ruprecht Wimmer, 228–53 (Frankfurt am Main: Klostermann, 1993).

THEMATIC STUDIES

A tirade against *Death in Venice* that rejects Mann's theory of art and finds his attitude toward pederasty immoral is Bernd Isemann, *Thomas Mann und Der Tod in Venedig: Eine kritische Abwehr* (Munich: Bonsels, 1913). According to Ernst A. Schmidt, "'Platonismus' und 'Heidentum' in Thomas Manns 'Tod in Venedig,'" *Antike und Abendland* 20.2 (1974): 151–78, Aschenbach briefly synthesizes the extremes of intellect and sensuality, in the treatise he writes at the beach, but he otherwise succumbs to the latter, perverting Plato's notion of love. Hermann Luft, *Der Konflikt zwischen Geist und Sinnlichkeit in Thomas Manns "Tod in Venedig"* (Bern: Lang, 1976), similarly argues that Aschenbach, as an artist, can only temporarily resolve the conflict between intellect and sensuality. Logos and Eros—Aschenbach's writing and his love for Tadzio—are structurally equated, according to Frederick Alfred Lubich, *Die Dialektik von Logos und Eros im Werk von Thomas Mann* (Heidelberg: Winter, 1986). A Dutch thesis—John Luijs, "Der Tod in Venedig von Thomas Mann: Rezeption des homoerotischen Elements" (Utrecht, 1987)—tells how critics and scholars accept or reject the homoerotic element in Mann's story. Karl Werner Böhm, *Zwischen Selbstsucht und Verlangen: Thomas Mann und das Stigma Homosexualität* (Würzburg: Königshausen & Neumann, 1991), likewise recounts the reception of the novella by describing the various views of this sexual element. J. M. Hawes, *Nietzsche and the End of Freedom* (Frankfurt am Main: Lang, 1993), argues that Mann had a different notion of Dionysus than Nietzsche and that he pits Nietzsche's psychology against Nietzsche's own aestheticism. Martina Hoffmann, *Thomas Manns "Der Tod in Venedig": Eine Entwicklungsgeschichte im Spiegel philosophischer Konzeptionen* (Frankfurt am Main: Lang, 1995), maintains that Aschenbach cannot live like Plato's Socrates or Nietzsche's Dionysus; instead, he negates the will to life, as Schopenhauer recommends, transcending this world en route to a higher one. The narrative role of mute gazes in Mann's story is the subject of John R. Frey, "'Die stumme Begegnung': Beobachtungen zur Funktion des Blicks im *Tod in Venedig*," *German Quarterly* 41.2 (March 1968): 177–95. Graham Good, "The Death of Language in *Death in Venice*," *Mosaic* 5.3 (Spring 1972): 43–52, says that Aschenbach is seduced by the music of language and abandons its sense.

The most complete account of Mann's setting of Venice, and of its treatment in other literary texts, is Bernard Dieterle, *Die versunkene Stadt: Sechs
Kapitel zum literarischen Venedig-Mythos* (Frankfurt am Main: Lang, 1995).

STYLISTIC STUDIES

Hermann Broch, "Philistrosität, Realismus, Idealismus der Kunst," *Der
Brenner* 3.9 (1 February 1913): 399–415, argues that the novella achieves
a Platonic equilibrium between realism and idealism, and that its style
recalls that of a musical composition. Bruno Frank, "Thomas Mann: Eine
Betrachtung nach dem 'Tod in Venedig,'" *Die Neue Rundschau* 24 (1913):
656–69, says that the novella attests to Mann's narrative discipline, which
is a formal counterweight to the kind of intoxication that kills Aschenbach. D. H. Lawrence, "German Books," *The Blue Review* 1.3 (July 1913):
200–206, sees in the novella a craving, for literary form, reminiscent of
Gustave Flaubert. Vernon Venable, "Poetic Reason in Thomas Mann,"
Virginia Quarterly Review 14 (Winter–Autumn 1938): 61–76, explains
Mann's symbols, contending that they become artfully ambiguous, syn-
thetic, and synoptic. Mann's ambiguous symbolism is likewise stressed in
Benno von Wiese, *Die deutsche Novelle von Goethe bis Kafka* (Düsseldorf:
Bagel, 1956). According to Oskar Seidlin, "Stiluntersuchung an einem
Thomas Mann-Satz," *Monatshefte* 39.7 (November 1947): 439–48, the
choice and arrangement of the words Mann uses in the first sentence of
his second chapter characterize Aschenbach's work and relatively unim-
portant life. Similarly, Fritz Martini, *Das Wagnis der Sprache* (Stuttgart:
Klett, 1954), focuses on the end of Mann's second chapter, contrasting
his narrator's freedom with his hero's fate, intellect with the destructive
forces of life. Dorrit Cohn, "The Second Author of 'Der Tod in Venedig,'"
in *Probleme der Moderne*, ed. Benjamin Bennett, Anton Kaes, and William
J. Lillyman, 223–45 (Tübingen: Niemeyer, 1983), distances Mann from
his moralistic narrator, remarking that the latter does not appreciate what
Aschenbach experiences. In André von Gronicka, "'Myth Plus Psychology': A Style Analysis of *Death in Venice*," *Germanic Review* 31.3 (October 1956): 191–205, Mann is said to have combined psychology and myth,
the real and the transcendent. In Walter Jens, *Statt einer Literaturgeschichte*
(Pfullingen: Neske, 1957), several of Mann's characters are said to embody the Greek god Hermes. Isadore Traschen, "The Uses of Myth in
'Death in Venice,'" *Modern Fiction Studies* 11.2 (Summer 1965): 165–79,
shows how Mann used myth in an ironic and parodistic way. Erich Heller,
Thomas Mann: The Ironic German (Boston: Little, Brown; London: Secker

& Warburg, 1958), tells how irony and parody indicate Mann's moralism. Walter Weiss, *Thomas Manns Kunst der sprachlichen und thematischen Integration*, Beiheft zur Zeitschrift "Wirkendes Wort" 13 (Düsseldorf: Schwann, 1964), demonstrates how Mann integrates the language and themes of his story. Hans W. Nicklas, *Thomas Manns Novelle "Der Tod in Venedig"* (Marburg: Elwert, 1968), also shows how well Mann's narrative structure integrates his motifs. David Luke, Introduction to *Death in Venice and Other Stories*, trans. David Luke, vii–li (New York: Bantam, 1988), tells how brilliantly Mann weaves together the elements of his story; it also decries the many mistakes made in H. T. Lowe-Porter's translation.

COMPARATIVE STUDIES

Hans Wysling, "Aschenbachs Werke: Archivalische Untersuchungen an einem Thomas Mann-Satz," *Euphorion* 59.3 (1965): 272–314, tells how Mann planned but never finished all of the works attributed to Aschenbach in the first sentence of the novella's second chapter. In Peter Heller, "Der *Tod in Venedig* und Thomas Manns *Grund-Motiv*," in *Thomas Mann: Ein Kolloquium*, ed. Hans H. Schulte and Gerald Chapple, 35–83 (Bonn: Bouvier, 1978), one reads that Mann's novella, like his other short fiction, conveys his fundamental theme: that culture and civilization are defeated by the drives of sex and death. Rolf Günter Renner, *Das Ich als ästhetische Konstruktion: "Der Tod in Venedig" und seine Beziehung zum Gesamtwerk Thomas Manns* (Freiburg im Breisgau: Rombach, 1987), argues that, in the novella as well as his other works, Mann constructed his ego in the biographies of his characters. The best of the many comparisons drawn between *Death in Venice* and *Tonio Kröger* (1903) is Richard Sheppard, "*Tonio Kröger* and *Der Tod in Venedig*: From Bourgeois Realism to Visionary Modernism," *Oxford German Studies* 18–19 (1989–90): 92–108. Mann's many quotations of *Death in Venice* in his other writings, and of those other writings in the novella, show his solidarity with his hero, according to Gert Bruhn, *Das Selbstzitat bei Thomas Mann* (New York: Lang, 1992). For a critique of Mann's own remarks on his story, one showing how they conflict and make it seem simpler than it is, see Herbert Lehnert, "Thomas Mann's Interpretations of *Der Tod in Venedig* and their Reliability," *Rice University Studies* 50.4 (Fall 1964): 41–60. Franz H. Mautner, "Die griechischen Anklänge in Thomas Manns 'Tod in Venedig,'" *Monatshefte* 44.1 (January 1952): 20–26, notes Mann's allusions to ancient Greece and parallels with passages in Homer and Plato. According to E. L. Marson, *The Ascetic Artist: Prefigurations in Thomas Mann's*

"*Der Tod in Venedig*" (Bern: Lang, 1979), both Euripides' *Bacchae* and Plato's *Phaedrus* are "prefigurative" models for Mann's story, which is analogous to the first and parodies the second. Ernst A. Schmidt, "Künstler und Knabenliebe: Eine vergleichende Skizze zu Thomas Manns *Tod in Venedig* und Vergils zweiter Ekloge," *Euphorion* 68.4 (1974): 437–46, compares that story to Virgil's second eclogue; both link art with pederasty. *Death in Venice* is compared to Goethe's *Die Wahlverwandtschaften* (Elective Affinities, 1809), and Mann's style is said to be a dualistic, ironic parody of Goethe's, in R. Hinton Thomas, "*Die Wahlverwandtschaften* and Mann's *Der Tod in Venedig*," *Publications of the English Goethe Society*, n.s., 24 (1955): 101–30. *Death in Venice* and Joseph Conrad's *Heart of Darkness* (1899) are contrasted in Lionel Trilling, "On the Modern Element in Modern Literature," *Partisan Review* 28.1 (January–February 1961): 9–35. One of the many comparisons drawn between Mann's novella and André Gide's *L'immoraliste* (The Immoralist, 1902) is in Kenneth Burke, *Counter-Statement* (New York: Harcourt, Brace, 1931). Renate Werner, *Skeptizismus, Ästhetizismus, Aktivismus: Der frühe Heinrich Mann* (Düsseldorf: Bertelsmann, 1972), claims that *Death in Venice* refers and replies to Heinrich Mann's *Die Göttinnen* (The Goddesses, 1902) and that Mann criticizes the aestheticism described by his brother. Similar, socially critical parallels between the novella and Heinrich's *Professor Unrat* (1905) are drawn in Walter H. Sokel, "Demaskierung und Untergang wilhelminischer Repräsentanz: Zum Parallelismus der Inhaltsstruktur von *Professor Unrat* und 'Tod in Venedig,'" in *Herkommen und Erneuerung: Essays für Oskar Seidlin*, ed. Gerald Gillespie and Edgar Lohner, 387–412 (Tübingen: Niemeyer, 1976).

HISTORICAL STUDIES

Heinrich Mann, "Der Tod in Venedig: Novelle von Thomas Mann," *März* 7.13 (29 March 1913): 478–79, interprets *Death in Venice* as an implicit political and social critique of Wilhelminian Germany. As noted above, in chapter 4, Georg Lukács, *Auf der Suche nach dem Bürger*, in Lukács's *Thomas Mann*, 9–48 (Berlin: Aufbau, 1949), does so, too, arguing that Mann reveals Aschenbach's "Prussian" ethic of composure to be extremely brittle. Inge Diersen, *Untersuchungen zu Thomas Mann* (Berlin: Rütten & Loening, 1959), another study by a Marxist scholar, calls Aschenbach typical of the bourgeois class in imperial Germany, not least because, in his barbaric intoxication at the end of Mann's story, he anticipates the bourgeois-imperialist tendency to fascism. To learn how

Mann's many allusions to historical details undermine the artistic time-lessness that writers like his hero strive to attain, see Herbert Lehnert, "Historischer Horizont und Fiktionalität in Thomas Manns *Der Tod in Venedig*," in *Wagner—Nietzsche—Thomas Mann: Festschrift für Eckhard Heftrich*, ed. Heinz Gockel, Michael Neumann, and Ruprecht Wimmer, 254–78 (Frankfurt am Main: Klostermann, 1993). As noted above, again in chapter 4, Hans Rudolf Vaget, "Thomas Mann und die Neuklassik: 'Der Tod in Venedig' und Samuel Lublinskis Literaturauffassung," *Jahrbuch der deutschen Schillergesellschaft* 17 (1973): 432–54, regards the influence of Samuel Lublinski and of early twentieth-century German neoclassicism in Mann's story. Franz Maria Sonner, *Ethik und Körperbeherrschung: Die Verflechtung von Thomas Manns Novelle "Der Tod in Venedig" mit dem zeitgenössischen intellektuellen Kräftefeld* (Opladen: Westdeutscher Verlag, 1984), ties that story to the "intellectual force field" of its time and thus explains Aschenbach's aesthetic ethics. Harvey Goldman, *Max Weber and Thomas Mann: Calling and the Shaping of the Self* (Berkeley: University of California Press, 1988), describes the death of Aschenbach's artistic personality according to Max Weber's sociological concept of the calling. For remarks linking Mann's account of cholera with the history of medicine and European imperialism, see Laura Otis, *Membranes: Metaphors of Invasion in Nineteenth-Century Literature, Science, and Politics* (Baltimore: Johns Hopkins University Press, 1999). Yahya Elsaghe, *Die imaginäre Nation: Thomas Mann und das "Deutsche"* (Munich: Fink, 2000), maintains that *Death in Venice* at once sexualizes the foreign, making it seem feminine, and describes cholera according to colonial European notions of Asia.

PSYCHOANALYTICAL STUDIES

According to Hanns Sachs, "Das Thema 'Tod,'" *Imago* 3.5 (October 1914): 456–61, *Death in Venice* is narrated like dreams that psychoanalysts interpret. Mann sublimates and displaces onto his hero his Oedipal and other conflicts, says Heinz Kohut, "'Death in Venice' by Thomas Mann: A Story About the Disintegration of Artistic Sublimation," *Psychoanalytic Quarterly* 26.2 (1957): 206–28. A patient undergoing psychoanalysis first felt threatened but then also felt relieved by his similarity to Aschenbach, reports Riva Novey, "The Artistic Communication and the Recipient: 'Death in Venice' as an Integral Part of a Psychoanalysis," *Psychoanalytic Quarterly* 33.1 (1964): 25–52. Peter Dettmering, *Dichtung und Psychoanalyse* (Munich: Nymphenburger Verlagshandlung, 1969), stresses Aschenbach's suicidal impulses. Harry Slochower, "Thomas Mann's *Death in Venice*," *American Imago* 26.2 (Summer 1969): 99–122, shows far greater appreciation of Mann's style and literary technique than most psychoanalysts' interpretations of his story. A reading that examines, in terms borrowed from C. J. Jung, his account of pedophilia and individuation, is given in Louis Zinkin, "'Death in Venice'—A Jungian View," *Journal of Analytical Psychology* 22.4 (October 1977): 354–66. A remarkable study of Mann's novella, one that is psychoanalytical and truly literate, and that applies ideas of Alfred Adler (1870–1937), is found in D. E. Oppenheim, *Dichtung und Menschenkenntnis* (Munich: Bergmann, 1926). For one of several discussions about whether Mann had actually read Freud when he wrote *Death in Venice*, see Wolfgang F. Michael, "Thomas Mann auf dem Wege zu Freud," *Modern Language Notes* 65.3 (March 1950): 165–71. Both Mann's supposed use of Freud and the sexual interpretations of his story by American readers are bemoaned in Allan Bloom, *The Closing of the American Mind* (New York: Simon and Schuster, 1987). For a survey of psychoanalytical readings of *Death in Venice*, consult Susanne Widmaier-Haag, *Es war das Lächeln des Narziß: Die Theorien der Psychoanalyse im Spiegel der literaturpsychologischen Interpretationen des "Tod in Venedig"* (Würzburg: Königshausen & Neumann, 1999).

STUDIES OF ADAPTATIONS IN OTHER MEDIA

David I. Grossvogel, "*Death in Venice*: Visconti and the Too, Too Solid Flesh," *Diacritics* 1.2 (Winter 1971): 52–55, rejects Visconti's film *Morte a Venezia* (1971) as too sexual and mundane, and neither symbolic nor subjective enough. The film is more gently judged in Jean Améry, "Venezianische Zaubereien: Luchino Visconti und sein 'Tod in Venedig,'" *Merkur* 25 (1971): 808–12, which accepts it, though its images seem less intellectual than Mann's words. Superficial similarities and profound differences between the novella and the film, which diminishes Mann's story in many ways, are noted in Werner and Ingeborg Faulstich, *Modelle der Filmanalyse* (Munich: Fink, 1977). Gabriele Seitz, *Film als Rezeptionsform von Literatur* (Munich: tuduv, 1979), argues that Visconti failed to adapt his literary model faithfully. In Béatrice Delassalle, *Luchino Viscontis "Tod in Venedig"* (Aachen: Shaker, 1994), however, the film, like the book, is judged a masterpiece. In his opera *Death in Venice* (1973), Britten uses both music and dance to convey Aschenbach's speechlessness, says Donald Mitchell, "*Death in Venice*: The Dark Side of Perfection," in *The Britten Companion*, ed. Christopher Palmer, 238–49 (Cambridge: Cambridge

University Press, 1984). Praise for the equivalence of Britten's music and libretto to Mann's words is bestowed in Peter Evans, *The Music of Benjamin Britten* (Minneapolis: University of Minnesota Press; London: Dent, 1979). Myfanwy Piper, "Writing for Britten," in *The Operas of Benjamin Britten*, ed. David Herbert, 8–21 (New York: Columbia University Press, 1979), tells how its author remained true to Mann's story when she wrote that libretto. According to Gary Schmidgall, *Literature as Opera* (New York: Oxford University Press, 1977), the opera, through the medium of music, improves on what even Mann was able to write.

Index

About the Author

ELLIS SHOOKMAN is Associate Professor of German at Dartmouth College. His previous books include *Eighteenth-Century German Prose* (1992), *The Faces of Physiognomy* (1993), *Noble Lies, Slant Truths, Necessary Angels: Aspects of Fictionality in the Novels of Christoph Martin Wieland* (1997), and *Thomas Mann's Death in Venice: A Novella and Its Critics* (2003).